THE PARISH COUNCILLOR'S GUIDE

The
Parish Councillor's Guide

The law and practice of parish, town and community
councils in England and Wales

by

PAUL CLAYDEN

EIGHTEENTH EDITION

 Shaw & Sons

Published by
Shaw & Sons Limited
Shaway House
21 Bourne Park
Bourne Road
Crayford
Kent DA1 4BZ

www.shaws.co.uk

First published 1922

Eighteenth Edition .... June 2003

ISBN 0 7219 0516 1

A CIP catalogue record for this book is available from
the British Library

Printed in Great Britain by
Bell & Bain Limited, Glasgow

CONTENTS

Contents

Contents

vii

Contents

Contents

Contents

Contents

Contents

Contents

Contents

PREFACE TO THE EIGHTEENTH EDITION

For over eighty years *The Parish Councillor's Guide*, under a series of editors, has attempted to meet the queries of generations of parish councillors and their clerks.

Although it is only three years since the previous edition, some important changes in the law have taken place. The Local Government Act 2000 abolished the surcharging of councillors for incurring unlawful expenditure and the criminal sanctions for failing to declare pecuniary interests. In their place, all councils have been required to adopt a code of conduct which all councillors must undertake to observe. Breach of the code can, in extreme cases, lead to suspension or disqualification from membership of the council. A Standards Board has been established in England to police the conduct of councillors, a function performed in Wales by the Commission for Local Administration (the local ombudsman). The model code of conduct for parish councils is printed in Appendix 1.

Under the Freedom of Information Act 2000, all local authorities (including not only parish councils but also parish meetings in England where there is no council) are required to adopt a publication scheme for the types of information which they are obliged to make available to the public.

In England, arising out of the government's Rural White Paper published in 2000, the concept of "Quality" parish councils has been introduced, and in Wales the National Assembly has commissioned a study to look at the functions of community councils.

Just before the book went to press, new Accounts and Audit Regulations were promulgated, making changes in the way parish council accounts are prepared and audited.

Preface to the eighteenth edition

I would like to pay tribute to my predecessor as editor, John Prophet, who was at the helm for more than twenty-five years. He brought to the task a wide and deep knowledge of parish law and was a legal consultant to the National Association of Local Councils for many years.

Parish councils are some of the great survivors among our governmental institutions. They were the only councils not abolished by the Local Government Act 1972, albeit reconstituted as community councils in Wales, and have now been in existence for more than 108 years. Long may they prosper as an admirable example of the benefits to our governmental system of local decision-making by elected representatives of the people.

Paul Clayden

EXPLANATION OF TERMS

Unless otherwise stated:

"parish council" means a parish council in England, a community council in Wales and a town council in either;

"parish meeting" means a parish meeting in England, a community meeting in Wales and a town meeting in either;

"parish" means a parish in England and a community in Wales;

a reference to a district or unitary council in England includes a county or county borough council in Wales.

In England, central government has various powers in relation to parish councils. Those powers are mostly exercised by the First Secretary of State. In Wales, the powers formerly exercised by the Secretary of State for Wales have been transferred to the National Assembly for Wales. In this book, the Secretary of State means the First Secretary of State in England unless otherwise stated and the National Assembly for Wales in Wales, or both, according to the context.

"D.E.F.R.A." means the Department for Environment, Food and Rural Affairs.

"O.D.P.M." means the Office of the Deputy Prime Minister; he is the First Secretary of State.

EXPLANATION OF THE FOOTNOTES

References to Acts of Parliament, Statutory Instruments and court cases are given in the footnotes for those readers who wish to refer to relevant sources.

Acts of Parliament which have been amended or modified may be noted by the phrase "as amended". Many of the Acts are given abbreviations of title followed by the year in which they received the Royal assent.

The full titles of these Acts and other abbreviations are given below and on the next page:

Art .... Article of a Statutory Instrument
r. .... Rule of a Statutory Instrument
Reg. .... Regulation of a Statutory Instrument
s. or ss. .... Section or Sections of an Act
Sch. .... Schedule to an Act or Statutory Instrument
S.I. .... Statutory Instrument

A.A. 1922 .... Allotments Act 1922
A.A. 1925 .... Allotments Act 1925
A.A. 1950 .... Allotments Act 1950
A.C.A. 1998 .... Audit Commission Act 1998
C.A. 1968 .... Countryside Act 1968
Ch.A. 1993 .... Charities Act 1993
C.J.P.O.A. 1994 .... Criminal Justice and Public Order Act 1994
C.R.O.W.A. 2000 .... Countryside and Rights of Way Act 2000
H.A. 1980 .... Highways Act 1980
H.P.A. 1986 .... Housing and Planning Act 1986
L.G.A. 1894 .... Local Government Act 1894
L.G.A. 1958 .... Local Government Act 1958
L.G.A. 1972 .... Local Government Act 1972
L.G.A. 1974 .... Local Government Act 1974
L.G.A. 1986 .... Local Government Act 1986
L.G.A. 1988 .... Local Government Act 1988
L.G.A. 1999 .... Local Government Act 1999
L.G.A. 2000 .... Local Government Act 2000
L.G.F.A. 1988 .... Local Government Finance Act 1988
L.G.F.A. 1992 .... Local Government Finance Act 1992

Explanation of the footnotes

ABSENCE FROM MEETINGS

(*See* Disqualifications for Office of Parish Councillor)

ACCEPTANCE OF GIFTS

(*See* Property of Parish Council)

ACCEPTANCE OF OFFICE

(*See* Parish Councillor)

ACCIDENTS

(*See* Insurance)

ACCOUNTS

(*See also* Audit—Books and Documents—Expenses and Expenditure—Inspection of Documents—Inspection of Parish Property—Value Added Tax)

Every parish council must make arrangements for the proper administration of its financial affairs and must secure that one of its officers is responsible for the administration of those affairs.[1] He is known as the responsible financial officer (RFO). (*See also* "Treasurer".) In practice, the clerk is usually appointed as RFO. It is the duty of the RFO to determine the form and content of the council's accounts and supporting records, subject to any directions from the council and to compliance with the Accounts and Audit Regulations 2003.[2] The RFO must ensure that the accounts and records are maintained in accordance with proper practices and kept up to date.[3]

---

[1] L.G.A. 1972, s. 151.
[2] The 2003 Regulations apply only in England. Comparable regulations for Wales will no doubt be made by the National Assembly for Wales.
[3] A.C.A. 1998, s. 2 and Accounts and Audit Regulations 2003 (S.I. 533).

1

Accounts

The accounts must be made up to the 31st March in each year and must be prepared in compliance with the 2003 Regulations. They prescribe different requirements for different categories of council as follows:-

1. Councils with a gross income or expenditure (whichever is the higher) for the year, and for each of the two immediately preceding years, not exceeding £100,000, or £100,000 or more for the year and the preceding year but not exceeding £500,000, must produce:

    (i) a record of receipts and payments of the council or meeting in relation to that period; or

    (ii) an income and expenditure account and a balance sheet of the council or meeting in relation to that period.

2. Councils with a gross income or expenditure (whichever is the higher) of £100,000 or more, but not exceeding £500,000, for the year and for each of the two immediately preceding years must produce an income and expenditure account and a balance sheet of the council or meeting in relation to that period.

3. Councils with a gross income or expenditure (whichever is the higher) for the year and for each of the two immediately preceding years of £500,000 or more must produce a statement of accounts on the same basis as principal authorities. The main requirements are to prepare the following: an explanatory introduction; summarised statements of the income and expenditure of each fund for which separate accounts are kept; a summarised statement of capital expenditure; a statement of accounting policies; a consolidated revenue account; a consolidated balance sheet; a consolidated cash flow statement; notes to the accounts, including corresponding figures for the previous financial year.

Once the accounts have been prepared, the RFO must sign and date them and must certify that they present fairly the financial position of the council for the relevant accounting period. Once signed, dated and certified, the accounts must be approved by resolution of the council or of a relevant committee (e.g. a finance committee). The approval is to be given as soon as practicable after the period to which it relates and in any event within six months after the end of the period.

The approved accounts must be audited and publicised (*see* "Audit").

All cheques must be signed by two councillors.[1] It is a good practice for cheques to be signed at the meeting of the council or committee at which the relevant accounts for payment are authorised. It is also good practice for cheque counterfoils to be signed or initialled by the cheque signatory as a guard against fraud or falsification. Cheques should never be signed in blank.

As to the accounts of a charity administered by the council, *see* "Charities".

Where a council makes a grant or loan, or provides a guarantee, to a voluntary body exceeding £2,000, it must require from that body a statement setting out the way in which the money has been applied.[2] This can readily be done by the body supplying the council with a copy of its annual report and accounts.

Parish council accounts must be open to inspection by any member of the council at all reasonable times without payment. Obstruction of such inspection is punishable with a fine not exceeding level one on the standard scale (currently £200). (*See* "Inspection of documents".)

---

[1] L.G.A. 1972, s. 150(5).
[2] L.G.A. 1972, s. 137A (inserted by L.G.H.A. 1989).

ACCUMULATION OF FUNDS

(See Funds and Accumulations)

ACQUISITION OF LAND

(See Compulsory Purchase of Land—Property of Parish Council)

ACTIONS

(See Legal Proceedings)

ACTS, LOCAL

(See Bills in Parliament—Local Act Powers)

ADMISSION OF PUBLIC TO COUNCIL MEETINGS

(See Meetings of Parish Council)

ADVISORY COMMITTEES

(See Committees)

AGENCY

(See *also* Committees—Joint Committees)

There is a general power[1] for a county or district council to transfer the administration of any statutory function, except those of levying a rate, issuing a precept, borrowing money or approving a scheme for local lotteries, to a parish council by mutual agreement. Since the statutory function remains one

---

[1] L.G.A. 1972, s. 101.

which is vested in the principal council and the function itself is not transferred (only its administration or discharge), it follows that the parish council is acting as an agent for the principal council. Consequently the principal council remains responsible for the expenses involved. Indeed, the principal council can continue to exercise the function notwithstanding the arrangement although this would be liable to cause confusion in practice.

Furthermore, a parish council exercising any function, whether directly or as an agent, may arrange for the discharge of the function by a committee, a sub-committee or an officer, but again this does not prevent the council from itself continuing to administer the function. Any committee may itself arrange for the discharge of a function by a sub-committee or officer, unless the council otherwise directs and similarly any sub-committee may arrange for the discharge of any function by an officer with the same proviso. (*See* "Committees".)

These are purely administrative arrangements and do not affect the basic responsibility of the authority upon which the function is granted by statute to ensure the proper performance of the function.

AGENDA

(See Meetings of Parish Council)

AGREEMENTS WITH OTHER PARISH COUNCILS

(See *also* Agency—Joint Committees—Lighting— Parking Places—Roadside Seats and Shelters)

A parish council may agree with any other parish council to discharge any of its functions jointly, and this may be done by a joint committee or by an officer of one of the councils.[1] Clearly this involves mutual agreement both with regard to the administrative arrangements and to the contributions which each authority will make to any capital or revenue expenditure.[2] In the case of joint committees only, if any dispute occurs on the apportionment of the expenses *of the committee*, this can be settled by the district council.[3]

This power may usefully be resorted to, for example, in the acquisition of a right of way in another parish or the acquisition of land for a recreation ground or swimming pool.

AGRICULTURAL HOLDINGS

(See Allotments)

ALLOTMENTS

(See *also* Compulsory Purchase of Land—Loans to Parish Council)

Parish Councils have power to provide allotments for personal cultivation, and have a *duty* to do so where there is an unsatisfied demand.[4] They must on this point consider any written representations by six parliamentary electors or ratepayers resident in the parish.[5]

A parish council is not bound to provide allotments other than allotment gardens.[6] The term "allotment garden" means an allotment not exceeding forty poles, i.e. 1,210 square yards,

---

[1] L.G.A. 1972, s. 101(5).
[2] L.G.A. 1972, s. 136.
[3] L.G.A. 1972, s. 103.
[4] S.H.A.A. 1908, s. 23(1).
[5] S.H.A.A. 1908, s. 23(2).
[6] A.A. 1950, s. 9.

in extent which is wholly or mainly cultivated by the occupier for the production of vegetable or fruit crops for consumption by himself or his family.[1] Allotments may not be sublet without the consent of the parish council.[2]

An allotment which is used for commercial cultivation may become an agricultural holding and thus subject to special rules as to notice to quit.

Formerly a separate account was required to be kept of allotments, and a surplus on this account could not be disposed of for other purposes without the consent of the Secretary of State. However, these requirements have now been abolished.[3] Nevertheless it remains advisable to keep a separate account in respect of allotments. Statutory allotment land, that is land purchased specifically for allotments purposes or formally appropriated for such use by a resolution of the council, must not be sold or appropriated for other purposes without the consent of the Secretary of State.[4]

Allotments are to be let at such rent as a tenant may reasonably be expected to pay, but a lower rent may be charged to a person if the council is satisfied that there exist special circumstances affecting that person which render it proper for it to let the land to him at a lower rent. Where the yearly rent exceeds £1.25, not more than a quarter's rent shall be payable in advance.[5]

Allotments are exempt from non-domestic rates.

The council may make rules for regulating the letting of allotments, defining the persons eligible to be tenants, the

---

[1] A.A. 1922, s. 22(1).
[2] S.H.A.A. 1908, s. 27(4).
[3] L.G.P.L.A. 1980, Sch. 5, para 2.
[4] A.A. 1925, s. 8, as amended.
[5] A.A. 1950, s. 10.

notices to be given for lettings, the size of allotments, the conditions under which they are to be cultivated, and the rents.[1] These rules no longer require the approval of the Secretary of State.[2] The council may appoint managers, who may be wholly or partly ratepayers who are not members of the council. Such managers may do anything which the council could do in regard to allotments, including the power to spend money. If they spend money, the expenses are deemed to be expenses of the local council.[3]

Rules make provision for reasonable notice to be given of the determination of a tenancy but if the rent for any allotment is in arrear for not less than 40 days, or if it appears to the council that not less than three months after the beginning of the tenancy the tenant has breached the rules, one month's notice to quit may be served on the tenant.[4] However, there are special statutory rules for allotments coming within the definition of an allotment garden and not attached to a cottage. The tenancy of such an allotment garden is not ordinarily to be terminable except by twelve months' notice to quit expiring on or before 6th April or on or after 29th September. Exceptions are re-entry after three months' written notice where the land is required for building, mining or other industrial purpose, for the purposes of a public undertaking or by the local authority for the purpose for which it was acquired; and re-entry for non-payment of rent or breach of any condition of the tenancy or on bankruptcy.[5]

In respect of an allotment garden not attached to a cottage, compensation for growing crops and manure is payable by the council if the tenancy is terminated by notice to quit, or

---

[1] S.H.A.A. 1908, s. 28.
[2] L.G.P.L.A. 1980, Sch. 5, para 1.
[3] S.H.A.A. 1908, s. 29.
[4] S.H.A.A. 1908, s. 30.
[5] A.A. 1922, s. 1, and A.A. 1950, s. 1.

by re-entry for any of the above-mentioned purposes after three months' notice. If the tenancy is terminated between 29th September and 11th October inclusive, the tenant has three weeks in which to remove the crops.[1]

Compensation for disturbance, in amount equal to one year's rent, is payable by the council in addition, where the tenancy is terminated by re-entry for any of the purposes mentioned above.[2]

Where the parish council is itself a tenant, it may recover compensation from the head lessor in similar circumstances to those outlined in the foregoing two paragraphs.[3]

Where the tenant of an allotment garden not attached to a cottage quits the land on the termination of the tenancy, the council may recover compensation from the tenant equal to the cost of making good any deterioration of the land caused by the failure of the tenant to maintain it clean and in a good state of cultivation and fertility.

In respect of all other allotments, compensation is payable on termination of the tenancy for whatever cause. The compensation is for growing crops and manuring and for fruit trees or bushes, drains, outbuildings, pigsties, fowlhouses or other structural improvements provided by the tenant with the previous consent in writing of the council. Compensation is determinable, in default of agreement, by a valuer appointed by the judge of the county court.[4] Before the termination of his tenancy a tenant may remove any fruit trees or bushes or any erection, fencing or other improvement provided by him for which he has no claim to compensation, making good any injury caused by the removal.[5]

---

[1] A.A. 1922, s. 2.
[2] A.A. 1950, s. 3(1).
[3] A.A. 1922, s. 2(6).
[4] A.A. 1922, s. 3.
[5] S.H.A.A. 1908, s. 47.

A parish council may let allotments to persons working on a co-operative basis.[1] If the council is of the opinion that the facilities from a society on a co-operative basis are inadequate, it may purchase fruit trees, seeds, plants, fertilisers or implements required for the purposes of allotments cultivated as gardens, whether provided by the council or otherwise, and sell any such articles to the cultivators or, in the case of implements, allow their use at a charge sufficient to cover the cost.

A parish council must be watchful that allotments are not used for purposes other than cultivation, and if necessary take steps to have any buildings, e.g. garages, removed.

If a council wishes to increase rents, it may do so at any time by agreement with the tenant. However, if the council is *imposing* an increase it must remember that it cannot do so within the period necessary for a notice to quit. It should therefore serve a formal notice to quit for the proper period on the tenant together with an offer of a new tenancy at the new rent immediately after that period, which the tenant should be asked to accept in writing. An accompanying letter can explain that the notice to quit is a formality to enable the rents to be increased.

Advice should be taken on problems arising in respect of allotments which were originally provided under inclosure Acts or awards, e.g. fuel allotments, or under the Poor Law.

For provisions as to compulsory purchase or compulsory hiring of land for allotments, *see* "Compulsory Purchase of Land".

Most of the powers of a parish council are concurrent with those of the district council. The provision of allotments is, however, an exception. A district council in England has no

---

[1] S.H.A.A. 1908, s. 27(6).

direct power to provide allotments in a parish.[1] However, in Wales a county or county borough council has a concurrent power with a community council.

ALLOWANCES TO PARISH COUNCILLORS

(See *also* Chairman of Parish Council (for chairman's allowance))

Members of the council, and co-opted members of committees of the council, are entitled to receive payment[2] when they carry out certain "approved duties" (*see below*) outside the parish. *No allowances* are payable for duties performed *within* the parish.

(a) Travelling allowances,[3] which may be either the actual cost of travel by public transport, or allowance for travel by the member's own car, up to a maximum rate laid down by the Secretary of State unless the approved duty was abroad in which case the amount is determined solely by the council itself.

(b) Subsistence allowance,[4] not exceeding the maximum rates laid down by the Secretary of State with the same qualification for an approved duty abroad as mentioned in respect of travelling allowances.

(c) Attendance allowance,[5] for councillors only (i.e. not for co-opted members of committees), as payment for the performance of an "approved duty", being a payment of

---

[1] L.G.A. 1972, Sch. 29, para. 9(1).
[2] The amount of the maximum payment is specified in Allowances Regulations made by the Secretary of State. These are regularly updated.
[3] L.G.A. 1972, s. 174.
[4] *ibid*.
[5] L.G.A. 1972, s. 173.

such reasonable amount as the council itself determines, subject to a ceiling in the form of an amount prescribed by the Secretary of State in regulations. The amount of the allowance may vary as to the time of day and the duration of the duty, but it must be the same for all members of the council entitled to the allowance in respect of a duty at the same time and of the same duration. The attendance allowance, being payable as of right, is taxable, and therefore must be declared to the Inland Revenue as income under Schedule E. In the case of members of committees who are not entitled to attendance allowance, not being councillors of that authority,[1] there is, in substitution for the attendance allowance, a financial loss allowance,[2] where for the purpose of performing an "approved duty" the member has necessarily suffered a loss of earnings which he would otherwise have made, or incurred additional expense (other than expense on travelling or subsistence, dealt with above) to which he would not otherwise have been subject. The amount of the allowance must not exceed the actual loss, or the maximum laid down by the Secretary of State in regulations, whichever is the less. Financial loss allowance is not taxable.

A councillor is entitled to opt for a financial loss allowance instead of receiving an attendance allowance. To do so, he must give to the council a notice in writing (a financial loss allowance notice) either within one month of his election, in which case it will apply from his election, or if not within that period then at any time thereafter, in which case it will operate after one month from the date of the notice.[3]

---

[1] *Hopson v. Devon County Council* [1978] 1 All E.R. 1205.

[2] L.G.A. 1972, s. 173.

[3] L.G.A. 1972, s. 173A as inserted by L.G.P.L.A. 1980, s. 24(2) and amended by the Miscellaneous Financial Provisions Act 1983, s. 7.

"Approved duty", in its application to a parish council, generally means in effect the doing of anything approved by the parish council, or anything of a class so approved, for the purpose of, or in connection with, the discharge of the functions of the parish council, or of any of its committees or sub-committees.[1] Thus it does not cover acting as a representative of the parish in matters in which the parish council has no function (even though the councillor may have been asked by the council to act). It does however include attendance as a representative of the parish council at certain conferences or meetings (*see* "Conferences").

A parish council may defray any travelling or other expenses of any member making an official or courtesy visit *on behalf of the council*, either at home or abroad. Unless the visit is abroad, the amount of any travelling or subsistence payments is subject to the limitations mentioned above.

A parish council may also pay for the expense of receiving, entertaining and informing distinguished visitors to the parish, and of persons representative of or connected with local government or public service in or outside the United Kingdom.

ALTERATION OF AREAS

(See *also* Grouping of Parishes—Name of Parish)

England

The Local Government Act 1992 established a new system for reviewing local government areas and altering boundaries. The Local Government Commission for England was created with overall responsibility for keeping local government areas and electoral arrangements under review. As a result of its

---

[1] L.G.A. 1972, s. 177(2).

recommendations, a number of so-called "unitary authorities" have been established which combine the functions of district and county councils. Some of these authorities are district councils to which the functions of the county council have been transferred and some are county councils to which the functions of the district council have been transferred. They are referred to in this book as "unitary councils".

The Local Government Commission was abolished in 2002 and its powers and functions were transferred to the Electoral Commission.

For parishes, the Local Government and Rating Act 1997 provides the statutory framework for reviewing areas and electoral arrangements. Reviews of parish arrangements are the responsibility of district and unitary councils. A review may cover the whole or part of the district or unitary council area and may recommend changes in parish boundaries (including the creation, alteration or abolition of a parish) and consequential changes in electoral arrangements. The Secretary of State may then accept (with or without modifications) or reject the recommendations or he may refer them to the Electoral Commission. If so referred, the Commission carries out a simplified review and reports back to the Secretary of State. He can then accept, modify or reject the Commission's recommendations. Once the review process is completed, any changes are implemented by order. Where the changes involve alterations to parish boundaries, or the abolition or creation of a parish, the order is made by the Secretary of State by statutory instrument. Changes in electoral arrangements are made by an order of the relevant district or unitary council.

It is expected that parish reviews will be undertaken about every 10 to 15 years, but there is no duty on the reviewing authorities to adhere to any particular timetable. The Secretary of State has power to direct a district or unitary council to carry out a review. He also has power to direct the Commission to carry out a parish review. In practice, the Secretary of State is unlikely to use these powers save on rare occasions.

The 1997 Act also introduced an entirely new procedure for creating parishes in unparished or partly unparished areas by way of petition. A petition may be presented to the district or unitary council requesting the creation of a parish and a parish council for a defined area. The petition must be signed by at least 250 or 10% of the local government electors in that area, whichever is the greater number. The receiving council must forward the petition to the Secretary of State. It has a right to add its comments but cannot block the petition. When he receives a petition, the Secretary of State may accept or reject it, or refer it to the Electoral Commission for review on the same basis as a recommendation from a district or unitary council.

Detailed guidance on parish reviews is contained in the Department of the Environment, Transport and the Regions' Circular 11/97 "Local Government & Rating Act 1997: Parish Reviews".

Wales

The Local Government (Wales) Act 1994 abolished the district and county councils and created new, single-tier, principal councils, called county councils or county borough councils, combining the functions of the abolished authorities. Community councils were largely unaffected by these changes.

The Local Government Boundary Commission for Wales is primarily responsible for reviewing principal local government areas and electoral arrangements in Wales. The county and county borough councils are responsible for reviewing community areas and electoral arrangements.

The whole of Wales is divided in to communities (not all of them with councils). There is thus no need for a mechanism to enable new communities to be created where none exist.

For the creation and dissolution of community councils, *see* "Parish Council – Creation of parish or community council *and* Dissolution of parish or community council".

Accretions

Every accretion from the sea, whether natural or artificial, and any part of the sea shore to the low water mark, is for all purposes of local government annexed to and incorporated with the parish or parishes which such accretion or part of the seashore adjoins.[1]

ANNUAL MEETING OF PARISH COUNCIL

(See also Meetings of Parish Council)

The parish council must, in every year, hold an annual meeting.[2] In a year involving the election of parish councillors the annual meeting must take place on the fourth day after the date of the election or within fourteen days thereafter. In other years it may be held on any day in May as determined by the parish council itself.[3] The annual meeting may be held at such time as the parish council decides, but if no hour is fixed it must begin at 6 p.m. in the evening.

In addition parish councils in England must hold at least three other meetings in the course of the year.[4] Community

---

[1] L.G.A. 1972, s. 72.

[2] L.G.A. 1972, Sch. 12, para. 7(1) and 23(1).

[3] *ibid.*, para. 7(2) and 23(2).

[4] *ibid.*, para. 8.

councils in Wales may hold such other meetings as they think fit.[1]

The first business at the annual meeting is the election of a chairman. (*See* "Chairman of Parish Council".)[2] There may also be elected a vice-chairman.

If the annual meeting is the first meeting after an election, the newly elected councillors should, if they have not done so before, make at that meeting in the presence of a councillor or the clerk, and deliver to the council, a declaration of acceptance of office in the prescribed form.[3] (*See* "Parish Councillor".)

The above arrangements and those set out in the note on "Meetings of Parish Council" are the principal statutory requirements in respect of the annual meeting. Other questions of procedure may be provided for in standing orders (*see* "Standing Orders") and otherwise are for determination by the chairman at the meeting.

For annual meeting of parish meetings, *see* "Parish Meeting".

APPROPRIATION OF LAND

(See Property of Parish Council)

APPROVED DUTY

(See Allowances to Parish Councillors)

ARCHIVES

(See Books and Documents)

---

[1] L.G.A. 1972, Sch. 12, para. 24.
[2] L.G.A. 1972, ss. 15 and 34.
[3] L.G.A. 1972, s. 83.

ARMISTICE DAY WREATHS

(See Free Resource)

ART GALLERIES

(See Museums and Art Galleries)

ARTS, THE

(See Entertainment and the Arts)

AUDIT

(See *also* Inspection of Documents—Joint Committees)

The accounts of the parish council are audited once in every year as soon as may be after 31st March by an auditor appointed by the Audit Commission. The auditor will either be a member of the Commission's staff or a private professional firm.[1]

The duty of the auditor is to see that the accounts have been prepared in accordance with legal requirements and to see that proper accounting practices have been observed in the compilation of the accounts. In addition he has a duty to consider whether, in the public interest, he should make a report on any matter arising out of, or in connection with, the accounts, in order that the matter should be considered by the council or brought to public attention.[2] If he makes such a report, he must send a copy to the Audit Commission[3] and there is a right of public inspection.[4]

---

[1] A.C.A. 1998, s. 3.
[2] A.C.A. 1998, s. 8.
[3] A.C.A. 1998, s. 10.
[4] A.C.A. 1998, s. 13.

An auditor has no power himself to judge whether the council has, or has not, acted within its powers. The former powers of an auditor of disallowance and surcharge have gone. If an auditor considers that any item of account is contrary to law, he may apply to the court for a declaration to that effect.[1] In addition to a declaration, the court may order rectification of the accounts.

No councillor, officer or any person acting under the council's direction has any personal liability in respect of anything done *in good faith* for the purpose of any of the council's statutory functions.[2]

An auditor may issue an advisory notice to a parish council or to an officer of the council if he has reason to believe that a decision is about to be taken, or has been taken—(a) involving unlawful expenditure, (b) to adopt a course of action which would, if concluded, result in a loss or deficiency, or (c) to enter an item of account which is unlawful. The effect of an advisory notice is that the council or its officer must give the auditor notice (not exceeding 21 days) if it or he intend to pursue the course of action specified in the notice.[3] In effect, therefore, an advisory notice is a formal warning and should not be ignored.

The following notes relate the usual procedure where an auditor is appointed.

The responsible financial officer arranges with the auditor the date for the commencement of the audit. He must then give at least fourteen days' public notice[4] of the commencement of a period of fifteen full working days during which the

---

[1] A.C.A. 1998, s. 17(1).

[2] L.G.(M.P.)A. 1976, s. 39.

[3] A.C.A 1998, ss. 19A-19C.

[4] Copies of this form are available from Shaw & Sons Ltd.

accounts and documents relating thereto will be available for public inspection. The notice must specify the place at which, and the hours during which the accounts and other documents may be inspected, and also include the name and address of the auditor and the rights of local government electors in respect of the audit. The public notice may be given by advertisement (in which case the auditor must be immediately advised of the name and date of publication of the newspaper, together with a copy of the notice) or by a notice in a conspicuous place in the parish (in which case the auditor must be immediately sent a certificate to that effect). The accounts and other documents must then be made available for inspection in accordance with the notice, and copies or extracts may be taken without charge. Where there are no accounts to be audited the chairman or clerk should certify accordingly to the auditor.

If the auditor decides to make a report on some matter, he must send a copy to the council and the Commission not later than fourteen days after the completion of the audit. The council must then convene as soon as possible to consider the report. Not later than fourteen days after that consideration the council must give public notice that the report is available for inspection, and allow for the taking of a copy thereof or an extract therefrom without payment.[1] Copies are to be *delivered* to any local government elector who so requests on payment of a reasonable sum for each copy.

Any local government elector for the parish is entitled to request the auditor to provide him with an opportunity to put questions to the auditor.[2] The elector is entitled to be present at the audit, or he may be represented at the audit and may make objection to the accounts at the audit.[3]

---

[1] A.C.A. 1998, s. 14(1).
[2] A.C.A. 1998, s. 15(2).
[3] A.C.A. 1998, s. 16(1).

The auditor, on the application of any person aggrieved by his decision on any matter with respect to which that person has made an objection, or of any person aggrieved by a certification by the district auditor that a sum is due from him, must state in writing the reasons for his decision, within six weeks of notification.[1]

Any person aggrieved by a decision of the district auditor on any matter with respect to which he made an objection at the audit may appeal to a court of law.[2] The court, on such an appeal, may confirm, vary, or quash the auditor's decision.

The Audit Commission may at any time either at the request of an elector or a council, or on its own initiative direct an auditor to hold an extraordinary audit of any of the accounts of a parish council. Also the Secretary of State may direct the Commission to do this.[3]

Fees for audits are prescribed by the Audit Commission, which has power to alter the prescribed fee in any case where the work done is less or more than that envisaged by the scale. At present parish councils are charged at an hourly rate.

The Audit Commission may give directions to certain local authorities requiring them to publish information as to their performance. The Secretary of State may by order bring parish councils within the ambit of that power.[4]

BANKRUPTCY

(See Disqualifications for Office of Parish Councillor)

---

[1] A.C.A. 1998, ss. 17(4).
[2] A.C.A. 1998, ss. 17(5).
[3] A.C.A. 1998, s. 25(1) and (2).
[4] L.G.A. 1992, s. 1 and s. 4.

BATHS, WASH-HOUSES, SWIMMING POOLS AND BATHING PLACES

(*See also* By-laws—Life-Saving Apparatus—Recreation)

A parish council may, either within or without the parish, provide public baths and wash-houses, open or covered, and with or without drying grounds;[1] and public swimming pools and bathing places, open or covered.[2] The power to provide wash-houses includes the power to provide launderettes. The power to provide buildings or other premises includes the power to equip them with such furniture, apparatus and instruments as may be necessary.[3]

With the consent of the Secretary of State loans may be raised for new provision or for the reconstruction of existing provision. (*See* "Loans to Parish Council".)

If necessary, a parish council requiring land for this service may obtain compulsory powers by an order of the district council confirmed by the Secretary of State. (*See* "Compulsory Purchase of Land".)

The council may make such charges for the use of, or admission to, any baths or wash-houses under its management as it thinks fit.[4] Notice of intention to consider a table of charges and naming a place where a copy may be inspected, must be advertised in a local newspaper at least a month before fixing any charges. Facilities at swimming pools or bathing places may be provided free or for such charge as the council considers appropriate.[5]

The council may make by-laws (subject to confirmation by

---

[1] P.H.A. 1936, s. 221(a).
[2] L.G.(M.P.)A. 1976, s. 19.
[3] L.G.A. 1972, s. 111.
[4] P.H.A. 1936, s. 222.
[5] L.G.(M.P.)A. 1976, s. 19.

the Secretary of State) for the regulation of any baths, wash-houses, swimming pools, etc. under its management, and for the regulation of persons resorting thereto, including the exclusion of undesirable persons.[1] (*See* "By-laws".)

Between the first of October and the last day of April, a parish council may close any swimming pool or bathing place under its management and use or let it for such purposes as it thinks fit and it may adapt it for those purposes.[2] The parish council may also close it temporarily at any time in order to grant exclusive use to a school or club for swimming purposes.[3]

The council may provide, lay down and maintain pipes and apparatus for conducting water to or from any baths, wash-houses, swimming pools or bathing places under its management, or which it proposes to provide, subject to certain restrictions relating to the breaking open of streets.[4]

Trustees of any public baths, wash-houses, etc. are empowered, with the consent of the committee of management (if any), to sell or lease the baths, wash-houses, etc. to a parish council.[5]

The district council may likewise provide baths, wash-houses, swimming and bathing places under these provisions. The parish council, instead of making provision itself, may contribute towards the expenses of another local authority or of a voluntary organisation in making such provision. Similarly, another local authority may contribute to expenses for this purpose of the parish council.[6]

Water, gas or electricity undertakers may supply water, gas or

---

[1] P.H.A. 1936, s. 223.
[2] P.H.A. 1936, s. 226.
[3] P.H.A. 1936, s. 225.
[4] P.H.A. 1936, s. 227.
[5] P.H.A. 1936, s. 228.
[6] L.G.(M.P.)A. 1976, s. 19.

electricity to any public baths, wash-houses, etc., either without charge or on such other favourable terms as they think fit.[1]

BENEFIT OF THE AREA

(*See Free Resource*)

BEST VALUE

Under the Local Government Act 1999, a few parish councils (those with an annual budget of £500,000 or more in England or £1 million or more in Wales) are subject to the "best value" regime. This means that they have to apply the principles of "best value" to their activities. They are under a duty to:-

(a) consult local people;

(b) review all functions periodically;

(c) measure their performance; and

(d) produce a performance plan which will be audited by an independent auditor.

Although the duty will apply to a small number of parish councils as a matter of law, the government expects all parish and town councils to embrace best value principles and follow best value practices as far as possible.

The Local Government Act 1999 requires best value authorities to make arrangements to secure continuous improvement in the delivery of their services, in the light of the following best value themes:-

(a) ensuring that public services are responsive to the needs of citizens, not the convenience of service providers;

---

[1] P.H.A. 1936, s. 229.

(b) ensuring that public services are efficient and of high quality;

(c) ensuring that policy making is more joined-up and strategic, forward looking and not reactive to short-term pressures;

(d) using information technology to tailor services to the needs of users;

(e) valuing public services and tackling under-representation of minority groups.

At the time of writing (April 2003), there were 41 parish and town councils in England subject to the "best value" regime and none in Wales.

BICYCLE PARKS

(See Parking Places)

BILLS IN PARLIAMENT

(See *also* Local Act Powers)

A parish council does not have the power, so important to other local authorities, of from time to time promoting a Bill in Parliament. However, a parish council now has a general power to oppose any local or personal Bill in Parliament.[1]

Powers may be conferred on parish councils by local Acts promoted by other local authorities, e.g. county councils. A parish council may press its county council to include desired powers in its next local Bill. In so far as powers under local Acts in force on the 1st April 1974 have not been preserved

---

[1] L.G.A. 1972, s. 239.

by general or local legislation or by local orders since the 1st April 1974, they expired in metropolitan counties at the end of 1979 and elsewhere at the end of 1984.[1] This does not, however, apply to local Acts passed after the 1st April 1974.

BOATING POOLS AND LAKES

(See Recreation)

BOOKS AND DOCUMENTS

Custody

The parish council may give directions as to the custody of all public books, writings, and papers of the parish,[2] excepting the registers of baptisms, marriages, and burials, and other books and documents containing entries wholly or partly relating to the affairs of the church or to ecclesiastical charities. The expression "affairs of the church" includes the distribution of offertories or other collections made in any church.

The incumbent and churchwardens on the one hand and the parish council on the other, shall have reasonable access to all such books, documents, writings and papers in the possession of the other. Any difference as to their custody or such access shall be determined by the county council.

It is the duty of the county council (in Wales, the county or county borough council), from time to time, to inquire into the manner in which the public books and documents under the control of the parish council are kept. That council may make orders for their preservation, and these orders must be complied with by the parish council.[3]

---

[1] L.G.A. 1972, s. 262.
[2] L.G.A. 1972, s. 226.
[3] L.G.A. 1972, s. 226(5).

Any local government elector of the parish may, without payment, inspect the minutes of the parish council at all reasonable hours and make a copy thereof.[1] He may inspect, also without payment, and make a copy of any order or the payment of money made by the council. The accounts of the council and of the treasurer shall be open to the inspection of any member of the council and any such member may make a copy thereof. (As to the deposit of books and accounts, etc. prior to audit and their availability for inspection by any person interested, *see* "Audit".) (*See also* "Inspection of Documents".)

Deposit

Various documents are required by statute or by standing orders of Parliament to be deposited with the proper officer, i.e. the clerk of the parish council—e.g. maps, plans, and sections of proposed works.[2] If there is no clerk, the documents must be deposited with the chairman of the council. Subject to any enactment to the contrary, a person interested in any such document may inspect the same, and take a copy thereof, on payment of 10p for the inspection, and a further sum of 10p for every hour the inspection continues beyond the first hour.[3]

In general terms, any requirement that a parish council shall keep a document of any description is satisfied if it keeps a photographic copy of the document.[4]

Depository

The parish council is required to provide proper depositories for all the documents, books and papers belonging to the parish or community for which no provision is otherwise made; or, if the local council so requests, the district council must

---

[1] L.G.A. 1972, s. 228.
[2] L.G.A. 1972, s. 225.
[3] L.G.A. 1972, s. 228(5).
[4] L.G.A. 1972, s. 229.

provide such depositories.[1] In practice many local councils have deposited their documents—other than those still required for current work—with the County Record Office. In many cases this will be the best way of ensuring the preservation of records which may ultimately be of value for local history.

Destruction[2]

Books, papers and documents of permanent value, such as minute books, ledgers, income registers, staff records; and all contracts, briefs and other important papers, relating to the sale and purchase of land and actions or proceedings affecting lands, should not be destroyed.

Treasurer's books; cash books and petty cash books; wages and salaries books; receipts, invoices and cheques; VAT records; contracts for works, except where there are special reasons for preservation; financial statements and loan statements; stock and store-books and rental books—may be destroyed when over six years old.

Counterfoil books; order check books; agenda books; postage books; pay cards and time sheets; tenders for goods, etc. may be destroyed on the expiration of twelve months from the completion of the audit of the last entry contained in the records.

Election papers may be destroyed on the expiration of the statutory period of six months after the election.

The above list is, of course, not exhaustive. Obsolete forms, out-of-date law books, year books, periodical journals of no permanent interest, and other such miscellaneous papers may be destroyed. The County Record Office will be able to advise in cases of doubt what records are worth retaining as of future historical interest.

---

[1] L.G.A. 1972, s. 227.

[2] This section represents best practice rather than legislative requirements.

Publication

Some parish councils have records of great historical interest. The Local Government (Records) Act 1962 gives parish councils wide powers to publish such records, hold exhibitions of them, and generally make them available for study by local historians and others.

As to signing and sealing documents, see "Parish Council".

BORROWING POWERS OF PARISH COUNCIL

(See Loans to Parish Council)

BOUNDARY CHANGES

(See Alteration of Areas)

BRIDLEWAYS

(See Footpaths—Highways)

BUILDINGS

(See Property of Parish Council)

BURIAL AND CREMATION

(See *also* Closed Churchyards—Expenses—Joint Committees—Loans to Parish Council—Mortuaries and Post-Mortem Rooms—Open Spaces)

A parish council (and an English parish meeting where there is no parish council) is a burial authority.[1] As such a parish

---

[1] L.G.A. 1972, s. 214.

council may provide, or contribute towards the provision of, a cemetery or crematorium. Land may be purchased by agreement or compulsorily.[1] Burial boards, joint burial boards and joint burial committees as existing on the 31st March 1974, ceased to exist on that date. However, if two or more burial authorities were involved they were obliged to set up a new joint board[2] or a joint committee.[3] (*See* "Joint Committees".)

Parish councils operate under the code based on an order made by the Secretary of State under the Local Government Act 1972. This is the Local Authorities' Cemeteries Order 1977, as amended by the Local Authorities' Cemeteries (Amendment) Order 1986.[4] Grounds hitherto maintained as burial grounds are now held as cemeteries.

The location of a cemetery very much affects the services and amenities of a local area. Thus at an early stage in the formulation of a scheme, the parish council should consult the planning authority. (*See* "Planning Permission".) The advertisement procedure in the Town and Country Planning Act 1990 applies to applications for planning permission to use land as a cemetery.

The powers of the parish council as burial authority include the provision of a crematorium.[5] A number of parish councils may combine for this purpose. The Secretary of State must first approve the plans and site and before use the council must certify to the Home Secretary that the building has been properly completed and equipped.[6] Regulations controlling

---

[1] L.G.A. 1972, s. 125 (as substituted by H.P.A. 1986, s. 43) and Sch. 26, paras. 7-9. For Compulsory Purchase procedure see p. 58 *post*.
[2] Under P.H.A. 1936, s. 6.
[3] L.G.A. 1972, Sch. 26, paras. 2 and 3.
[4] 1977, S.I. 204 and 1986, S.I. 1782.
[5] Cremation Act 1902, s. 4.
[6] Cremation Act 1952, s. 1 as amended by L.G.P.L.A. 1980, s. 188.

cremation have been made by the Home Secretary under the Cremation Acts 1902 and 1952. More people are now cremated than buried every year in Britain.

A chapel may be erected on the cemetery at the expense of the parish council,[1] and the council may lay out and embellish the grounds of the cemetery as it thinks fit.[2]

The parish council may, if it thinks fit, apply to the bishop for consecration of a cemetery.[3] A fee is payable. Only part of the ground should be consecrated.

The parish council determines the fees to be charged.[4] A table of fees must be kept, and be available for public inspection. Non-parishioners have no right of burial but are usually allowed burial on payment of a higher scale of fees. The fees payable to ministers of religion or sextons may be fixed by the burial authority. An exclusive right of burial can no longer be sold in perpetuity, but only for a fixed period not exceeding 100 years, subject to extension for up to 100 years from the date on which the extension is granted.[5] Such a right may be granted under the signature of the clerk of the council. No seal is necessary.[6]

A burial authority must keep the cemetery in good order and repair and may remove tombstones and kerbs after giving proper notice if there are no objections.[7] Vandalism in

---

[1] Local Authorities' Cemeteries Order 1977, Art. 6 (which also provides for denominational chapels to be provided by the parish council at the expense of the denomination).

[2] *ibid.*, Art. 4.

[3] *ibid.*, Art. 5.

[4] *ibid.*, Art. 15.

[5] *ibid.*, Art. 10. (The Order provides a procedure for determining rights already granted for a period greater than 75 years but unexercised for 75 years from the date of the grant.)

[6] *ibid.*, Schedule 2.

[7] *ibid.*, Art. 4, Art. 16 and Sch. 3.

31

cemeteries is an offence.[1]

The keeping of a register of burials is an essential requirement and so too is the keeping of a plan and register of purchased graves.[2]

Parish councils may contribute towards the expenses incurred by any other person in maintaining any place of interment in which the remains of inhabitants of the parish or community are or may be interred irrespective of the denomination of the owners.[3]

A council may, by agreement with any person, maintain any private grave or memorial for a period not exceeding 100 years.[4]

BUS SERVICES, SUPPORT OF

(See Transport)

BUS SHELTERS

(See *also* Roadside Seats and Shelters)

Local authorities, including parish councils, may provide and maintain shelters or other accommodation (e.g. seats at bus stops) for passengers by bus, coach, trolleybus or tram at stopping-places in highways within their districts or on any land abutting on such highways.[5] They may make with other local authorities or with transport operators agreements for the provision and maintenance of such shelters or other accommodation, and such agreements may provide for

---

[1] Local Authorities' Cemeteries Order 1977, Arts. 18 and 19.
[2] *ibid.*, Arts. 9 and 11.
[3] L.G.A. 1972, s. 214(6).
[4] Local Authorities' Cemeteries Order 1977, Art. 10.
[5] L.G.(M.P.)A. 1953, s. 4(1).

contributions by such other local authorities or operators towards the cost of such provision and maintenance.[1]

Either of the local authorities referred to above may be a parish council, so that the effect is to empower parish councils either to provide bus shelters themselves or to contribute towards the cost of shelters provided by other local authorities.

Where a shelter is to be erected on land abutting on a highway and the land is not already in the possession of the council, it will be necessary either to acquire the land or to obtain from the owner of the land the right to erect the shelter thereon. (*See* "Property of Parish Council" and "Compulsory Purchase of Land".)

The power to provide a shelter is subject to various consents.[2] The consent of the highway authority is required or that of railway or certain other transport undertakers in the case of certain highways repairable by those undertakers. Where the shelter is to be situated on, or on the approaches to, a bridge, the consent of the authority or other person in whom the bridge is vested is necessary. Where the shelter is to be situated on, or on the approaches to, a bridge carrying a highway over a railway, canal or inland navigation, or under a bridge carrying any of the foregoing over a highway, the consent of the undertakers concerned is necessary. In addition, where the shelter is to be situated so as to obstruct or interfere with any existing access to any land or premises abutting on the highway, the consent of the owner of the land or premises is required.

Any of these consents is not to be unreasonably withheld but may be given subject to reasonable conditions, which may include a condition that the council shall subsequently remove the shelter if reasonably required to do so. Any dispute between

---

[1] L.G.(M.P.)A. 1953, s. 4(2).
[2] L.G.(M.P.)A. 1953, s. 5 as amended by L.G.P.L.A. 1980, Sch. 7, para. 6(2).

a Minister whose consent is required (e.g. as highway authority for a trunk road) and a local authority as to whether the consent of that Minister is being unreasonably withheld is to be settled by arbitration.

Where a shelter is situated so as to obstruct access to telecommunication apparatus belonging to a telecommunications operator, or any sewer, pipe-subway, pipe, wire or other apparatus belonging to or maintained by a local authority or statutory undertaker, and the telecommunications operator or the authority or undertaker concerned gives notice requiring such access, the council shall temporarily remove the shelter or shall be liable to repay the extra expense incurred in obtaining access.[1] In view of this provision, and of statutory provisions imposing penalties for obstructing fire hydrants,[2] care should be taken in siting bus shelters to avoid obstructing access to any such apparatus.

Planning permission is not in general required for the erection of a bus shelter. (*See* "Planning Permission".)

A parish council may maintain shelters, or queue barriers or posts provided by them under Defence Regulations, or without statutory powers, or accepted as a gift prior to the 14th July 1953.[3] The provisions with regard to consents, and obstructions to access are applied to the maintenance of such shelters or barriers, subject to the modification that any necessary consent need not be obtained again if it was obtained when the shelter was first provided.

A parish council may borrow money for the provision of a bus shelter, subject to the usual consents. (*See* "Loans to Parish Councils".)

---

[1] L.G.(M.P.)A. 1953, s. 6 as amended by Telecommunications Act 1984, Sch. 4.

[2] Fire Services Act 1947, s. 14(5).

[3] L.G.(M.P.)A. 1953, s. 7.

BY-ELECTIONS

(*See* Election of Parish Councillors)

BY-LAWS

(*See also* Baths and Wash-Houses—Mortuaries and Post-Mortem Rooms—Open Spaces—Recreation— Village Greens)

A parish council may make by-laws for the following purposes:–

(i) the regulation of any pleasure ground or public walk, which is for the time being under its control, or to the expense of which it has contributed. The by-laws may provide for the removal from such ground, etc. of any person infringing any by-law, by any officer of the parish council or by a constable.[1]

(ii) the regulation of any open space or burial ground over which the parish council has acquired any interest or control by virtue of the Open Spaces Act 1906, including the days or times of admission thereto and the preservation of order and prevention of nuisances therein. The by-laws may provide for the removal of any person infringing any by-law by an officer of the parish council or by a constable.[2]

(iii) the regulation of any baths, swimming pools, bathing places or wash-houses provided by the parish council,[3] and swimming pools and bathing places not managed by the council and which are open to the public at a charge;[4]

---

[1] P.H.A. 1875, s. 164, and L.G.A. 1972, Sch. 14, para. 27.

[2] O.S.A. 1906, s. 15.

[3] P.H.A. 1936, s. 223.

[4] P.H.A. 1936, s. 233.

and the regulation of public bathing.[1]

(iv) the regulation of any mortuaries and post-mortem rooms provided by the parish council.[2]

(v) the regulation of the hiring of pleasure boats in a park or pleasure ground provided or managed by the council.[3]

(vi) to control dogs and dog fouling.[4]

Model by-laws for these purposes have been issued by the central government. Inquiries should be made to the Office of the Deputy Prime Minister, Democracy and Leadership Division, Eland House (5/B1), Bressenden Place, London SW1E 5DU.

The procedure for making by-laws is as follows.[5] By-laws are made under the hands and seals of two members of the parish council. They have no effect, however, until confirmed by the confirming authority, i.e. the Secretary of State. At least one month before application for confirmation, notice must be given of the intention to apply for confirmation, in one or more local newspapers. A copy of the by-laws must be deposited at the council offices, and be open to public inspection, without payment, for at least a month before application for confirmation.

The council must on application furnish to any person a copy of the draft by-laws, or any part thereof, on payment of such sum, not exceeding 10p for every hundred words, as it may determine.

---

[1] P.H.A. 1936, s. 231, as amended by L.G.(M.P.)A. 1976, s. 17, and L.G.A. 1972, Sch. 14, para 18.

[2] P.H.A. 1936, s. 198.

[3] P.H.A.A.A. 1890, s. 44(2); P.H.A. 1961, s. 54.

[4] P.H.A. 1875, s. 164; O.S.A. 1906, s. 15.

[5] L.G.A. 1972, s. 236.

A copy of the confirmed by-laws must be printed and deposited at the council offices and open at all reasonable hours to public inspection without payment, and a copy must be furnished on application to any person, on payment of such sum not exceeding 20p for every copy as the council may determine.

By-laws may also be made on matters for which a local council has no direct authority, e.g. against cycling on footpaths,[1] by a district council or a unitary council. A parish council could ask that council to process such a by-law on its behalf or to delegate to the parish council the power to make it.[2]

A copy of any by-law made by the above council must be transmitted to the clerk of the parish council of every local area to which such by-laws relate. In the case of a parish in England without a council, the copy must be sent to the chairman of the parish meeting. The copy of these by-laws must be deposited with the public documents of the local areas, and must be open to public inspection, without payment, at all reasonable times.

CAMPING AND CARAVANS

District councils and unitary councils in England and county and county borough councils in Wales have the power to prohibit the parking of caravans on commons.[3] It is unlawful for caravans to be parked on a village green. (*See* "Village Greens".)

Visiting touring caravans may not, in general, be parked on private land without a licence from the above council, but a

---

[1] L.G.A. 1972, s. 235.
[2] L.G.A. 1972, s. 101.
[3] Caravan Sites and Control of Development Act 1960, s. 23, and L.G.A. 1972, Sch. 29, para. 14.

single van may be parked without a licence for not more than two nights. A licence is not necessary for the parking of a limited number of vans if the site is approved by a recognised organisation such as the Caravan Club.

CAPITAL GAINS TAX

(See Income Tax)

CAR PARKS

(See Parking Places)

CASH

(See Accounts)

CASTING VOTE

(See Chairman of Parish Council—Chairman of Parish Meeting)

CASUAL VACANCY IN PARISH COUNCIL

(See Election of Parish Councillors)

CEMETERIES

(See Burial and Cremation)

CHAIRMAN OF PARISH COUNCIL

(*See also* Chairman of Parish Meeting)

Each year the parish council at the commencement of its annual meeting is required to elect the chairman of the council.[1] If the council is a town council, he is entitled to the style of Town Mayor.[2] His election must be the first business transacted. The chairman must be elected from the members of the council. At the meeting at which the chairman is elected (or before or at a later meeting, if so permitted by the council) he must make in the presence of a member of the council, or the clerk of the council, and deliver to the council, a declaration of acceptance of office in the form prescribed which includes an undertaking to observe the council's code of conduct in the performance of his duties.[3] If he fails to do so his office thereupon automatically becomes vacant. The chairman continues in office unless he resigns or becomes disqualified, until his successor becomes entitled to act as chairman. During his term of office the chairman continues to be a member of the council notwithstanding that he may not have been re-elected as a councillor. If this happens he only has a casting vote on the election of the new chairman.[4]

As to disqualifications for being chairman, *see* "Disqualifications for Office of Parish Councillor".

A parish council may pay the chairman for the purpose of enabling him to meet the expenses of his office such allowance as the council thinks reasonable.[5] Provided the amount paid is a reasonable reimbursement for expenses actually incurred, the allowance is not taxable. The amount must not, however, include any element of remuneration for the chairman.

The chairman may resign office by giving notice in writing to the council.[6] No acceptance by the council is necessary when

---

[1] L.G.A. 1972, ss. 15 and 34.
[2] L.G.A. 1972, s. 245.
[3] L.G.A. 1972, s. 83(4) as amended by L.G.H.A. 1989; L.G.A. 2000, s. 52(2). Form available from Shaw & Sons Ltd.
[4] L.G.A. 1972, s. 15(2).
[5] L.G.A. 1972, ss. 15(5) and 34(5).
[6] L.G.A. 1972, s. 84.

the chairman sends in his resignation; the office becomes vacant on the receipt of notice of the resignation by the council.

The chairman of the parish council may convene a meeting of the council[1] or a parish meeting[2] at any time. He may also be required to heed a request for him to call a meeting by councillors (*see* "Meetings of Parish Council"). Public notice of any parish meeting and of any parish council meeting must be given, and in the latter case a summons, signed by the clerk, must also be sent to each councillor. Seven "clear days" means days exclusive of the day of notice and the day of the meeting. (*See* "Notices".)

Where the voting at a meeting of the parish council is equal, the chairman, or the person presiding in his place, has a second or casting vote.[3]

The minutes of a council meeting must be signed at the same or the next ensuing meeting by the presiding chairman.[4] Any instrument to be executed by the council may be signed by the clerk on the council's behalf,[5] but if it is a document which requires a seal (e.g. a deed), it must be signed and sealed by two members of the council.[6]

Any notice required by law to be given to the chairman may be left at, or sent by post to, the offices of the council. (*See* "Notices".)

If the chairman of the parish council is present at any meeting, he must preside.[7]

---

[1] L.G.A. 1972, Sch. 12, para. 9(1) and 25(1).

[2] *ibid.*, para. 15(1)(a) and 30(1)(a).

[3] *ibid.*, para. 39(2).

[4] *ibid.*, para. 41(1).

[5] L.G.A. 1972, s. 234.

[6] L.G.A. 1972, ss. 14(3) and 33(3).

[7] L.G.A. 1972, Sch. 12, paras. 11(1) and 27(1).

The council may, if it thinks fit, appoint one of its number to be vice-chairman.[1] He holds office until immediately after the election of a chairman at the next annual meeting of the council, and during that time continues to be a member of the council for all purposes, notwithstanding that he may not have been re-elected as a councillor. The vice-chairman, in the absence or during the inability of the chairman to act, has all the powers and authority of the chairman; and, subject to any standing orders of the council, anything authorised to be done by, to, or before the chairman, may be done by, to, or before the vice-chairman.

CHAIRMAN OF PARISH MEETING

If the chairman of the parish council is present at a parish meeting, he is the chairman of the meeting. If, in England, he is absent, the vice-chairman (if any) shall, if present, preside. If neither is present, the meeting may appoint a person to take the chair, and that person will then have the powers and authority of the chairman for the purpose of that meeting.[2]

In Wales, the office of vice-chairman of the community council does not entitle the person holding that office to be chairman of the community meeting if the chairman of the council is absent, although in practice he would no doubt take the chair unless the meeting decided otherwise.

In England, where a parish does not have a separate parish council, the parish meeting shall, subject to the provisions of a grouping order, at its annual assembly elect a chairman who will then, unless he resigns in writing, remain in office for the year.[3] The chairman continues in office until his

---

[1] L.G.A. 1972, ss. 15(6) and 34(6).

[2] L.G.A. 1972, Sch. 12, paras. 17 and 33.

[3] L.G.A. 1972, s. 15(10).

successor is appointed. A casual vacancy in the office of chairman of the parish meeting is to be filled by the parish meeting.[1] In Wales, where a community does not have a separate community council, the meeting must appoint a chairman for the occasion only.[2]

Where the voting at a meeting is equal, the chairman has a second or casting vote.[3] A poll may be demanded before the conclusion of a meeting, on any question arising thereat. (*See* "Polls".)

Any notice required to be given to or served on a parish meeting may be given to or served on the chairman of the meeting.[4]

CHAPELS

(See Burial and Cremation)

CHARITIES

The law relating to charities is now mainly to be found in the Charities Act 1993.

A parochial charity is one where the benefits (or a separate distribution of benefits) are confined to inhabitants of the parish which includes the area of the present civil parish (or part of it) or of an area consisting of the parish with not more than four neighbouring parishes.[5]

The parish council (or in some cases, in England only, the parish meeting) may by statute appoint trustees for certain

---

[1] L.G.A. 1972, s. 88(3).
[2] L.G.A. 1972, Sch. 12, para. 33.
[3] *ibid.*, paras. 18(3) and 34(3).
[4] L.G.A. 1972, s. 231(2).
[5] Ch.A. 1993, s. 96(1).

parochial charities, in the circumstances listed below.[1] These powers are in addition to any powers of appointment conferred by a trust instrument. In no case do these include ecclesiastical charities.

(a) where before 1894 the inhabitants of the parish, the vestry or select vestry appointed trustees for (or beneficiaries of) a charity, the parish council shall appoint the trustees (or the persons who shall select the beneficiaries of the charity);

(b) where the churchwardens as such (before 1894) or the overseers as such (before 1894 or before 1927) were trustees, then the parish council shall appoint trustees to a not greater number than the former trustees;

(c) where the charity trustees of a charity not founded within the preceding forty years do not include persons elected by the electors, ratepayers or inhabitants or appointed by the parish council or parish meeting, the parish council or parish meeting may appoint such number of additional trustees as the Charity Commission may allow;

(d) where, in a case covered by (c) above, there is a sole charity trustee not so elected or appointed, the number of trustees may (with the approval of the Commission) be increased to three, one of the new trustees being appointed by the existing trustee and one by the parish council or parish meeting.

The term of office of first trustees appointed under these provisions is four years, except that where new appointments are made under (c) or (d) above and more than one trustee is appointed, half (as nearly as may be) must be for two years; and an appointment to fill a casual vacancy does not extend beyond the end of the term of the appointment it fills. Retiring trustees are eligible for re-appointment.[2]

---

[1] Ch.A. 1993, s. 79(2) and (5).
[2] Ch.A. 1993, s. 79(6).

Where trustees are appointed by the parish council, the council cannot itself administer the parochial charity. The trustees are an entirely different body from the parish council. Councillors may be appointed by the council as trustees, but if so they are acting as trustees, not as councillors.

The Act provides a valuable protection for a trustee in doubt as to how to execute his trust, in entitling him (on written application) to the advice of the Charity Commission.[1] The head office address of the Charity Commission is Harmsworth House, 13-15 Bouverie Street, London EC4Y 8DP. If he follows this he is protected against any action for breach of trust unless the matter had already been before the court or proceedings were pending, or he had reason to suspect that the advice was given in ignorance of material facts.

The Act also provides for co-operation between charities and the council.[2] Where the charity is established for a purpose similar or complementary to one of the council's services, the council may (if both parties wish) make arrangements with the charity for co-ordinating their work in the interest of the people served.

Trustees holding property for the purposes of a public recreation ground, or of allotments for the benefit of the inhabitants of the parish, or for any other charitable or public purposes connected with a parish—except for an ecclesiastical charity—may, with the approval of the Charity Commission, transfer the property to the parish council or to persons appointed by the council.[3] If the parish council accepts the transfer, the property will be held on the same trusts and subject to the same conditions as those under which the trustees held it.

---

[1] Ch.A. 1993, s. 29.
[2] Ch.A. 1993, s. 78.
[3] Ch.A. 1993, s. 79(1).

The Act further provides for a change in the area to which a charity relates in certain cases where the original area is no longer appropriate.[1]

Where a charity is administered by a parish council, the accounts of the parochial charity are usually audited by the council's auditor, the sums involved counting towards calculating the audit fee. Where, however, the council only appoints trustees of the charity, but does not itself administer it, the accounts of the charity are distinct from those of the parish council, and will neither form part of their accounts nor be subject to audit by the auditor.

The trustees of a charity are required to keep proper accounts and accounting records and must keep them for six years. The type of accounts to be kept are prescribed by regulations and depend upon the level of financial activity of the charity:-

1. For a charity with an annual income not exceeding £1,000 and without a permanent endowment or occupation or use of land, no specific form of accounts is prescribed, but they may be prepared as if the charity was in the next category; no audit is required.

2. For a charity with neither income nor expenditure exceeding £10,000, accounts must be prepared, but may be on a receipts and payments basis, together with a simple annual report; no audit is required.

3. For a charity with an income exceeding £10,000 but not exceeding £100,000, accounts must be prepared, but may be on a receipts and payments basis; the accounts must be subject to scrutiny by an independent person (not necessarily an auditor) and an annual report must be prepared; the accounts, report and annual return must be sent to the Commission.

---

[1] Ch.A. 1993, s. 13(4).

4. For a charity with income and expenditure exceeding £100,000 but not exceeding £250,000, the requirements are the same as for the previous category except that the accounts must be prepared on an accruals basis.

5. For a charity with income and expenditure exceeding £250,000 in the current year or either of the two previous years, the requirements are the same as for the previous category except that a full audit must be carried out by a qualified auditor.[1]

A trustee of a parochial charity, or his wife or children, cannot receive any benefit from the charity.

The draft of any scheme for the reform of an obsolete charity affecting the parish may be made by the Charity Commission and must be communicated to the parish council at least one month before the order is made.[2] Charities may apply for a scheme to enable them to invest their funds jointly by setting up a common investment fund.[3]

All charities, apart from certain "exempt" charities and some "excepted" by regulation, *must* be registered by their trustees with the Charity Commission, unless they have neither a permanent endowment, nor the use and occupation of land and whose income from all sources does not exceed £1,000 per year.[4] The effect of registration is to put beyond question the fact that the trust is charitable.

The Charities Act 1993 provides for the maintenance of local indexes of charities.[5] The indexes comprise extracts from the Central Register, maintained by the Charity Commissioners,

---

[1] Ch.A. 1993, Part VI.
[2] Ch.A. 1993, s. 20.
[3] Ch.A. 1993, s. 24.
[4] Ch.A. 1993, s. 3.
[5] Ch.A. 1993, s. 76.

covering charities which relate to the area of a local authority. The county council keeps an index and is entitled to free copies of any relevant entry in the Charity Commission's register. The county council has power to publish information contained in the index, and the index is open to public inspection. In county areas the index slips will be arranged according to the area in which the charity operates, so that where the area of benefit is made up of a number of parishes a separate slip will be found relating to each of the parishes.

The Act also provides for reviews of charities having the same or similar purposes to be made by county councils, but no charity can be reviewed without the consent of its trustees.[1]

For rating of charities, *see* "Rating and Valuation".

CHEQUES

(See Accounts)

CHURCHYARDS

(*See also* Closed Churchyards)

Where a churchyard is open, a parish council may contribute towards its maintenance. (*See* "Burial and Cremation".)

CITIZENS' ADVICE BUREAUX

A parish council may assist voluntary organisations to provide individuals with information about those individuals' rights and obligations. The council may also assist, by making or receiving communications or by providing representation

---

[1] Ch.A. 1993, s. 77.

before any person or body, in asserting those rights or fulfilling those obligations.[1]

In practice, this power is mostly used to provide financial assistance to Citizens' Advice Bureaux or similar organisations.

CLERK OF PARISH COUNCIL

(See *also* Agency—Deputy Officers—Employees— Gratuities to Officers—Legal Proceedings—Meetings of Parish Council—Parish Meeting—Superannuation of Paid Officers—Treasurer of Parish Council)

A parish council must appoint such officers as it thinks necessary for the proper discharge of its functions.[2] In addition a parish council must secure that one of its officers has responsibility for the administration of its financial affairs.[3] (*See* "Treasurer of Parish Council".) Thus a parish council may have an "executive and responsible financial officer" but, in practice, all frequently falls upon the modest "clerk".

A member of the parish council may be appointed to be clerk of the council without remuneration,[4] but it is nowadays more usual for the council to appoint some other suitable person, not being a councillor, to the post and to pay him or her such reasonable remuneration as it may determine. A person who has been a parish councillor may not be appointed as clerk *with remuneration* until twelve months have elapsed since he ceased to be a councillor.[5] The appointment of a clerk or other parish council officer is made by resolution of the council.

Whilst few clerks are likely to take on the responsibilities

---

[1] L.G.A. 1972, s. 142(2A).
[2] L.G.A. 1972, s. 112.
[3] L.G.A. 1972, s. 151, i.e. the responsible financial officer.
[4] L.G.A. 1972, s. 112(5).
[5] L.G.A. 1972, s. 116.

purely for the money, a reasonable remuneration ought to be paid to every clerk. In recent years the status of clerks has considerably improved and all councils should be prepared to examine the payment made to their clerks in the light of the not inconsiderable work and responsibility which falls to them. Advice may be obtained from the Society of Local Council Clerks, 1 The Crescent, Taunton, Somerset TA1 4EA.

Certain functions of the council must be carried out by the proper officer of the council which means the officer specifically appointed for that purpose. For most matters this will be the clerk, but when a council has more than one officer, for example a separate treasurer, that officer may well be appointed the proper officer for certain statutory purposes.

As proper officer, the clerk will be required to sign the summonses to attend meetings[1] (*see* "Meetings of Parish Council") but he has no power to fix the meetings of the council except in so far as he has the express or implied authority of the chairman to do so. The extent of his general authority over the council's affairs is governed by the wishes of the council.

The duties of the clerk will depend on the terms of his contract if he is an employee but will ordinarily include the duty of summoning and attending the meetings of the council; keeping the council minutes; taking charge of the council books and deeds and documents, and giving copies or extracts from the same to any person entitled, on payment of the prescribed or other reasonable charge for the same. If no separate treasurer is appointed he will also keep the accounts of the council and attend at the audit as may be required. As to whether it is part of his duty to take the minutes at parish meetings, *see* "Parish Meeting".

---

[1] L.G.A. 1972, Sch. 12, para. 10(2)(b).

Service of any notice upon a parish council may be effected by service upon the office of the authority,[1] i.e. in practice, its clerk.

As to deposit of documents with the clerk, see "Books and Documents".

An officer must not, under colour of his office or employment, exact or accept any fee or reward whatsoever other than his proper remuneration[2] although he is entitled to be reimbursed for all legitimate expenses.

If it comes to the knowledge of an officer that a contract in which he has any pecuniary interest, whether direct or indirect (not being a contract to which he is himself a party), has been, or is proposed to be, entered into by the council or any committee of the council, he must as soon as practicable give notice in writing of his interest to the council.[3] An officer is treated as having an indirect interest if he would have been so treated had he been a member. On this, *see* "Interest in Contract or Other Matters".

An officer of the council has no personal liability in respect of anything done *in good faith* for the purpose of any of the council's statutory functions.[4]

As an employee of the council, the clerk is covered by the legislation (now very extensive) dealing with employment rights, discrimination in employment, unfair dismissal, redundancy and similar matters (*see* "Employees").

A national training strategy for clerks has been launched by the National Association of Local Councils. Details can be

---

[1] L.G.A. 1972, s. 231.
[2] L.G.A. 1972, s. 117(2).
[3] L.G.A. 1972, s. 117(1).
[4] L.G.(M.P.)A. 1976, s. 39.

obtained from the Association at 109 Great Russell Street, London WC1B 3LD.

CLOCKS

(See Public Clocks)

CLOSED CHURCHYARDS

England

Any inhabitant of a parish, whatever his religion, is entitled to be buried in the churchyard.[1] Thus if a churchyard ceases to be usable, the Secretary of State may make representations to the Privy Council for an Order in Council discontinuing burials in a churchyard where he is satisfied that such a step is necessary for the protection of public health.[2] The parochial church council is responsible for the maintenance of the closed churchyard in decent order and for the necessary repairs to walls and fences.[3]

The parochial church council can at any time give three months' written notice to the parish council that it wishes the churchyard to be maintained at public expense.[4]

If the parish council prefers that the responsibility for maintenance should fall upon the district council rather than itself, it may within the three months so resolve and serve a further notice to this effect in writing upon the district council and the parochial church council. The district council is then obliged to take over the maintenance of the churchyard instead of the parish council at the end of the three months.[5]

---

[1] *Hughes v. Lloyd* (1888) 22 Q.B.D. 157.
[2] Burial Act 1853, s. 1.
[3] L.G.A. 1972, s. 215(1).
[4] L.G.A. 1972, s. 215(2).
[5] L.G.A. 1972, s. 215(3).

If it does not serve the further notice, the parish council will become responsible for the maintenance of the churchyard at the end of the three months, and the parish council cannot thereafter transfer the responsibility to the district council.

As a consequence of the Care of Churches and Ecclesiastical Jurisdiction Measure 1991 (in force from 1st March 1993), the responsibility for maintaining trees in a closed churchyard now falls on the council.

A parish council cannot be required to maintain a churchyard which is disused but not closed.

Wales

Before 1st April 1974, responsibility for the maintenance of closed churchyards could be transferred to the then parish councils and parish meetings. Any transfers which took place before that date remain effective. After that date, parishes were replaced by communities and the transfer procedure in section 215 of the Local Government Act 1972 does not apply in Wales. Community councils cannot therefore be required to take over maintenance of a closed churchyard. They may, however, contribute towards the cost incurred by any other person in so doing.[1]

The Care of Churches etc. Measure 1991 (see above) does not apply to the Church in Wales.

CODE OF CONDUCT

Every parish council is required to adopt a code of conduct, which must contain the mandatory provisions of the model

---

[1] L.G.A. 1972, s. 214(6).

code of conduct prescribed by the Secretary of State.[1] (In fact, all the provisions of the model code are mandatory.) Every member and co-opted member of a parish council must comply with the council's code of conduct. The prescribed form of declaration of acceptance of office which every newly elected or co-opted councillor must sign contains an undertaking to observe the code. The model code for parish councils in England is set out in Appendix 1. (There are no material differences between the English and Welsh model codes.)

Where a member has a prejudicial interest (defined in paragraph 9 of the model code), he must withdraw from the room where the meeting is being held, unless he has been granted a dispensation by the standards committee of the "responsible authority" (i.e. the district or unitary county council in England and the county or county borough council in Wales). A dispensation will in general only be granted where the parish council would otherwise be unable to come to a decision (e.g. where so many councillors have prejudicial interests that the council is inquorate).

Every principal authority must establish a standards committee. The general functions of the standards committee are to promote and maintain high standards of conduct by members and to assist members to observe the council's code of conduct. The standards committee of the relevant principal authority (district or unitary council in England; county or county borough council in Wales) performs the foregoing general functions in relation to the parish councils in the authority's area. Every such standards committee must include at least one parish or community councillor and at least one such councillor must be present at a standards committee meeting

---

[1] L.G.A 2000, s. 50; Parish Councils (Model Code of Conduct) Order 2001 (S.I. 3576); Conduct of Members (Model Code of Conduct) (Wales) Order 2001 (S.I. 2289).

when matters relating to the parish councils in the area are under consideration.

It is open to anyone to make a written allegation to the Standards Board (in England) or a Local Commissioner for Administration in Wales that a councillor has failed to observe the council's code of conduct.[1] An elaborate procedure is laid down for dealing with allegations of breaches of a council's code, the details of which are outside the scope of this book. If an allegation of breach of the code is proved, the councillor in question may be suspended or partially suspended (i.e. suspended only from performing particular functions or having particular responsibilities) for a period not exceeding one year or for the remainder of his term of office, if shorter. Alternatively, the councillor may be disqualified from office for up to five years.

COMMISSION FOR LOCAL ADMINISTRATION

A parish council is not subject to inquiry by the Local Commissioner for Administration, nor can it instigate an inquiry into any other local authority. Any such complaint has to be made by an individual person, who may complain to the Local Commissioner or to an elected member of that authority.

In Wales, the Commission for Local Administration performs the functions which in England are performed by the Standards Board.

COMMITTEES

(See also Joint Committees—Parish Meeting)

A parish council may arrange to discharge any of its functions

---

[1] L.G.A. 2000, ss. 58 and 69.

through a committee, or a sub-committee of the council.[1] In the view of the author, there is no reason why such a committee should not include all the members of the council, if that is the wish of the council but an executive committee of one is illegal.[2] Unless the council otherwise directs, any committee appointed by the council may itself arrange for the discharge of any of its functions by a sub-committee. It is not necessary for the full council to ratify committee decisions. The only powers which cannot be transferred to a committee are those of issuing a precept for a rate and of borrowing money. A committee (other than a finance committee) may include persons who are not members of the parish council.[3] Special rules for committees of local councils are to be found in the Parish and Community Councils (Committees) Regulations 1990. Every member of a committee who at the time of his appointment was a member of the parish council, upon ceasing to be a councillor, ceases also to be a member of the committee or sub-committee.[4]

If the parish council has any functions which are to be discharged in a part only of the parish, or in relation to a recreation ground, building, or property held for the benefit of a part only of the parish, the council may appoint a committee for that function.

Any arrangement made by a parish council for the discharge of any of its functions by a committee or sub-committee does not prevent the council or committee which made the arrangements from exercising these functions.

A parish council may also appoint an advisory committee in

---

[1] L.G.A. 1972, s. 101.
[2] *R. v. Secretary of State for the Environment ex parte Hillingdon London Borough Council* [1986] 2 All E.R. 273. It follows that the chairman can exercise no executive action on behalf of the council.
[3] L.G.A. 1972, s. 102(3), as amended by L.G.H.A. 1989, s. 13(8).
[4] L.G.A. 1972, s. 102(5).

respect of any matter relating to the discharge of any of its functions and there are no restrictions in membership of such committees. In fact it may consist entirely of non-members.[1] (*See* "Standing Orders".)

The parish council may make, vary and revoke standing orders respecting the quorum, proceedings and place of meeting of a committee or (with the other authorities concerned) a joint committee but, subject to any such standing orders, the quorum, proceedings and place of meeting shall be such as the committee or joint committee determine.[2] (*See* "Standing Orders".)

The public (which includes members of the Press) must be admitted to all committees of the parish council. In the case of sub- committees there is no obligation to admit the public, but it is advisable to do so since the public and the Press have a legitimate interest in the deliberations and decisions of all local authorities. (For exclusion of the public, see "Meetings of Parish Council".)

The chairman at any meeting of a committee or a joint committee has a second or casting vote.

Minutes of the proceedings of every committee must be kept. They should be submitted to the parish council, but only require the council's approval in so far as they relate to the exercise of powers or functions of the council which have not been transferred to the committee. (*See* "Inspection of Documents".)

The accounts of a committee form part of the accounts of the parish council and are to be audited as part of those accounts. For audit of joint committees, *see* "Joint Committees".

---

[1] L.G.A. 1972, s. 102(4).
[2] L.G.A. 1972, s. 106.

COMMON PASTURE

Where it appears desirable to acquire land for affording common pasture, a parish council may prepare and carry into effect a scheme for acquiring such land, provided that the land can be acquired at such price or rent that all expenses incurred may reasonably be expected to be recouped out of the charges paid in respect thereof.[1] Upon such a scheme being carried into effect the statutory provisions relating to allotments (e.g. the making of rules) will apply in like manner as if "allotments" in those provisions included common pasture, and "rent" included a charge for turning out an animal on the pasture. (*See* "Allotments".) Rules made by the parish council in respect of common pasture may extend to regulating the turning out of animals on the common pasture, defining the persons entitled to turn them out, the number to be turned out, and the conditions under which animals may be turned out, and fixing the charges to be made for each animal, and other-wise for regulating the management of the common pasture.

COMMONS

(*See also* Roadside Wastes—Village Greens)

Common land is land subject to rights of common, or manorial waste, registered as common land under the Commons Registration Act 1965. For the purposes of the Commons Registration Act, the term common land excludes village greens (although the latter were also registrable under the Act as a separate category). In earlier statutes, however, references to common land may be taken as including village greens.

District and unitary councils have powers to prevent the

---

[1] S.H.A.A. 1908, s. 34, as amended by L.G.A. 1972, Sch. 29, para. 9.

unlawful inclosure of commons.[1] A parish council should keep a careful watch on any common within the parish or community and make representations to the above council when any inclosure is threatened or has taken place.

A parish council which owns common land should be cautious in purporting to allow any person or body to do anything which may be unlawful. For example, a building or fencing of any kind on land subject to rights of common is unlawful without the consent of the Secretary of State.[2] Any person who camps or lights a fire on common land, or who drives a vehicle on to it, commits an offence if the common land is subject to s. 193 of the Law of Property Act 1925. In addition it is, in any event, an offence to drive a car on to a common more than 15 yards from the road,[3] although if the parish council owns the common, or can obtain the permission of the owner, a simpler expedient against unwanted parking is to dig a ditch or place large white stones on the boundary.

Under section 61 of the Criminal Justice and Public Order Act 1994, powers are given to the police to remove trespassers from land, if the trespassers are there for the purpose of residence (e.g. "travellers"). The power is exercisable if the trespassers have caused damage, or have used threatening, abusive or insulting words to the occupier, or if they have six or more vehicles with them on the land. The section applies specifically to common land. Where the public has access to such land, the local authority is treated as an occupier and may therefore ask the police to remove the trespassers. The local authority is the parish council, the district council, the county council or the unitary council; they have concurrent powers in this respect.[4]

---

[1] L.P.A. 1925, s. 194.

[2] *ibid.*

[3] R.T.A. 1988, s. 34.

[4] C.J.P.O.A. 1994, ss. 61, 62.

A parish council may agree to contribute the whole or any portion of the expense of a scheme prepared by the district or unitary council for the regulation and managment of any common within a parish or community under the Commons Act 1899 as amended by the Local Government, Planning and Land Act 1980.[1] Powers to make a scheme or to confer powers of management under such a scheme may be transferred to the parish council by the district council.[2]

Where common land is registered but has no registered owner, a parish council (and any other local authority in the area of which the common is situated) has power to protect the common from unlawful interference (e.g. trespass or encroachment) and may take legal proceedings for this purpose.[3]

A right of public access extends at present to about one fifth of registered common land by virtue of various statutes passed over the last 150 years. When Part 1 of the Countryside and Rights of Way Act 2000 comes into force (expected to be in 2005), a statutory public right of access on foot will apply to all registered common land.

COMMUNITY

In Wales, all rural parishes in existence immediately before the 1st April 1974 ceased to exist as local areas, but were reborn on that date under the name of communities. This name was also given in Wales to all former boroughs and urban districts in existence immediately before the 1st April

---

[1] L.G.P.L.A. 1980, s. 1(3) and Sch. 3 but note the possibility of the powers of the district council being taken over by the county council if there is no longer a district council.

[2] L.G.A. 1972, s. 101.

[3] Commons Registration Act 1965, s. 9.

1974, with a few adjustments involving some grouping of divided parts of former urban districts.[1]

Thus every part of Wales lies within a local area known as a community, in contrast to England where the effect of the change was that only the former rural parishes and certain free standing urban areas constitute the comparable local area known as a parish (*see* "Parish"). There is a right to convene a community meeting for any community in Wales (*see* "Parish Meeting"). A community meeting is not a corporate body and in most cases where there is no council, property is held on its behalf by the county or county borough council. (To compare the position in this respect in England, *see* "Parish Trustees".) Unless it is specifically stated to the contrary or the context indicates otherwise, any reference in this book to a "parish" should be taken as including a "community", and any reference to a "parish meeting" should be taken as including a "community meeting". It is hoped that Welsh readers will in no way take this amiss. It is done simply for ease and economy of expression.

COMMUNITY CENTRES

(See Village Halls)

COMMUNITY COUNCIL

(See Parish Council)

COMMUNITY MEETING

(See Community—Parish Meeting)

---

[1] L.G.A. 1972, s. 20.

COMPULSORY PURCHASE OF LAND

(*See also* Property of Parish Council)

In some cases, there are specific powers enabling parish councils to compulsorily purchase land for certain functions, e.g. allotments,[1] but generally if a parish council is unable to acquire by agreement and on reasonable terms suitable land for *any* purpose for which it is authorised to acquire land it may represent the case to the district or unitary council, and if that council is satisfied that suitable land cannot be purchased on reasonable terms by agreement, and that the circumstances are such as to justify it in proceeding with a view to compulsory purchase, it must hold a local inquiry into the representation of the parish council.[2] The district or unitary council is required to publish in the parish, in the manner prescribed[3] by the Secretary of State, notice of the inquiry and also to serve notice in the prescribed form on the owners, lessees and occupiers of the land proposed to be taken. After the inquiry has been completed and all objections by persons interested have been considered, the district or unitary council may make a compulsory purchase order, which cannot become effective until it is confirmed by the Secretary of State. The confirmed order is carried out by the district or unitary council, but the land itself is conveyed to the parish council.

If the district or unitary council refuses to make an order for the purchase of the land otherwise than by agreement, the parish council may petition the Secretary of State, who may, after holding a local inquiry, make a compulsory purchase order.

This power of a parish council to acquire compulsorily any

---

[1] S.H.A.A. 1908, ss. 25, 39.
[2] L.G.A. 1972, s. 125, as substituted by H.P.A. 1986, s. 43.
[3] The Compulsory Purchase of Land Regulations 1994, S.I. 2145.

land which is necessary for any of its functions is quite general. It is not limited by the fact that particular statutes confer powers of compulsory acquisition on local authorities except parish councils.

The word "land" in relation to any purpose for which the parish council is authorised to acquire land includes any interest in land, and any easement or right in, to, or over land.

The procedure on compulsory acquisition is governed by the provisions of the Acquisition of Land Act 1981.

Under the provisions of the Land Compensation Act 1961, as amended by the Planning and Compensation Act 1991, the price payable to the owner on compulsory acquisition is broadly speaking the market value of the land, estimated by the district valuer and determined in the event of dispute by the Lands Tribunal, but advice should be taken on the latest legal position in this respect.

The district or unitary council may make an order for the compulsory purchase of land for the purpose of letting it to a parish council for allotments. Such an order is subject to confirmation by the Secretary of State. (*See* "Allotments".)

CONCURRENT POWERS

All the powers of a parish council, with the exception of allotments in England, are concurrent with those of the district or unitary council.

CONFERENCES

A parish council may pay any councillor allowances for attendance at conferences or meetings. These allowances are attendance allowance or financial loss allowance and travelling and subsistence allowance (*see* "Allowances to Parish Councillors"). This applies to any conference or meeting which the council itself considers relates to the interests of its area or its inhabitants. The only exclusions are conferences which are convened in the course of trade or business or the objects of which are wholly or partly political. The council itself decides how many councillors may attend. There are no restrictions on the number of conferences which may be attended.[1]

Thus, any number of councillors may be authorised to attend meetings of County Associations and the national conference of the National Association of Local Councils.

CONSENT OF PARISH COUNCIL

Although there are now several cases where notice must be given to a council (*see* "Notices by or to Parish Council"), in the following case, the parish council is actually able to prevent another authority from carrying out a statutory function.

If a highway authority applies to a magistrates' court for authority to stop up or divert an unclassified road, including a footpath or bridleway, the highway authority must be able to satisfy the court that the relevant parish council has been advised and for a period of two months has not refused its consent. (*See* "Highways".)

It may also be noted here that no parish in England may be grouped without the consent of the parish meeting of each of the parishes. (*See* "Grouping of Parishes".)

---

[1] L.G.A. 1972, s. 175.

CONSENTS, ETC. UNDER THE PARISH COUNCILS ACT 1957

(See also Lighting—Parking Places— Public Clocks— Roadside Seats and Shelters)

The powers to provide roadside seats and shelters, public clocks and public lighting under the Parish Councils Act 1957, are subject to the provisions of that Act as to consents and access to telegraphic lines, etc.[1]

None of these things, nor any material or apparatus, is to be provided on any land or premises not forming part of a road or in a position obstructing or interfering with any existing access to any such land or premises, except with the consent of the owner and the occupier; or in any road which is not a highway or in any public path except with the consent of the owner and the occupier of land over which the road or path runs.

For the definition of "road", *see* "Roads".

Similarly, such provision in, or on land abutting on, any road which is a highway requires the consent of the highway authority (or the Secretary of State in the case of a trunk road or other road maintained by him). The consent of the undertakers concerned is also required where the provision is to be made in a road which is a highway belonging to and repairable by any railway, dock, harbour, canal, inland navigation or passenger road transport undertakers and forming the approach to any station, dock, wharf or depot of those undertakers; or on the approaches to any bridge carrying a highway over any railway, dock, harbour, canal or inland navigation, or under any bridge carrying a railway, canal or inland navigation over a highway.

---

[1] P.C.A. 1957, s. 5.

Any of these consents is not to be unreasonably withheld but may be given subject to reasonable conditions, which may include a condition that the council shall subsequently remove the thing provided if reasonably required to do so. Any disputes are to be settled by the Secretary of State (who may hold a local inquiry for the purpose) or, where he is one of the parties, by arbitration.

The provisions of section 6 of the Local Government (Miscellaneous Provisions) Act 1953, relating to access to telecommunication apparatus, sewers, etc. in the case of bus shelters, are applied also by section 5 of the Act of 1957, to the exercise of these powers (*see* "Bus Shelters").

CONSTABLES, PARISH

The office of parish constable was abolished by the Police Act 1964.

CONSULTATION

The Local Government and Rating Act 1997 and the Local Government Act 1972[1] provide that the Secretary of State may designate matters on which principal councils must consult parish councils in their area before a decision is made. No designations have yet been made, but the Secretary of State has indicated that there will be designations if principal councils do not voluntarily consult parish councils on a range of agreed matters. As a result, a considerable number of principal authorities have drawn up formal consultation agreements with the parishes and communities in their areas; these are sometimes called "charters" (*see also* "Quality Parish Councils"). These agreements do not affect any statutory rights of consultation which parish councils may have (*see* "Planning").

---

[1] L.G.R.A. 1997, s. 21; L.G.A. 1972, s. 33A, inserted by L.G.W.A. 1994, s. 14.

CONTRACTS OF PARISH COUNCIL

(See *also* Best Value—Interest in Contract or Other Matters— Officers of Parish Council—Standing Orders)

A parish council may enter into any contracts which are relevant to the discharge of any of its functions.[1] Apart from contracts for the sale or other disposition of land, which must be made in writing,[2] contracts may legally be made in any form.

A parish council may also make standing orders with respect to the making of contracts by the council. However it *must* make such orders with respect to contracts for the supply of goods or materials to the council, or for the carrying out of any works, which orders must include a provision for regulating the manner in which tenders are invited, but may exempt from any such provision contracts below a certain fixed price or generally where the council is satisfied that exemption is justified by special circumstances.[3]

Model standing orders are available from the National Association of Local Councils. (*See* "Standing Orders".)

CONTRACT WITH THE COUNCIL, INTEREST IN

(See Interest in Contracts or Other Matters)

CONVENING OF MEETINGS

(See Meetings of Parish Council—Parish Meeting)

---

[1] L.G.A. 1972, s. 111.
[2] L.P.(M.P.)A. 1989, s. 2.
[3] L.G.A. 1972, s. 135.

CO-OPTION

(See Election of Parish Councillors)

CORPORATION TAX

A parish council is not liable to Corporation Tax.

COUNCILLOR

(See Parish Councillor)

COUNCIL TAX

The council tax is the local tax payable in respect of the occupation of residential property. Parish councils, and parish meetings in England without a council, obtain most of their income by precepting on the billing authority (district or unitary council), which raises the money from the council tax payers in the parish area. Council tax bills show the amount raised in this way. (*See* "Precepts" and "Expenses and Expenditure".)

COUNTY ASSOCIATION OF PARISH OR LOCAL COUNCILS

(See National Association of Local Councils)

COUNTY COUNCIL, CONSENT OF

Many former restrictions on parish council powers in the nature of the need to obtain the consent of the county council have disappeared in recent years. Of the remaining ones, the most important relate to lighting powers (*see* "Lighting"), grass verges and traffic signs (*see* "Highways"), car parks (*see* "Parking Places") and public conveniences (*see* "Public Conveniences").

CREMATION

(See Burial and Cremation)

CRIME PREVENTION

A parish council may, for the detection or prevention of crime, (a) install and maintain any equipment (e.g. controlled circuit cameras), (b) establish and maintain any scheme (e.g. neighbourhood watch) and (c) assist others in undertaking the foregoing. The council may also make grants to the police authority for police purposes.[1]

The responsible authorities for each local government area (primarily county councils and unitary authorities) and the police must formulate a strategy for the reduction of crime and disorder in their area. They must co-operate with other bodies, including parish councils, in producing and implementing the strategy.[2] Parish councils must exercise their functions with due regard to the likely effect of such exercise on crime and disorder in their area and the need to prevent them.[3]

CUSTODY OF BOOKS

(See Books and Documents)

CYCLE PARKS

(See Parking Places)

---

[1] L.G.R.A. 1997, s. 31.
[2] Crime and Disorder Act 1998, s. 5; Crime and Disorder (Prescribed Descriptions) Order 1998 (S.I. 2452).
[3] Crime and Disorder Act 1998, s. 17.

DAMAGE

Damages recoverable by the parish council or parish meeting for damage caused by negligence to any lamp, lamp-post, notice board, fence, rail, post, shelter or other "apparatus or equipment provided by them in a street or public place" are recoverable in a magistrates' court as a civil debt if the amount does not exceed £20.[1] Above that figure proceedings should be taken in the county court.

On a prosecution for criminal damage, a magistrates' court can, on conviction, order the offender to pay up to £5,000 compensation in addition to any punishment inflicted.[2]

DECLARATION OF ACCEPTANCE OF OFFICE

(See Parish Councillor)

DECLARATION OF INTEREST

(See Code of Conduct)

DECLARATION THAT HIGHWAY IS UNNECESSARY

(See Highways)

DEDICATION OF HIGHWAY

(See Highways)

---

[1] P.H.A. 1961, s. 81 and Powers of Criminal Courts (Sentencing) Act 2000, s. 131.

[2] Magistrates Courts Act 1980, s. 40.

DELEGATION

(*See* Agency—Committees)

DEPOSITORY FOR BOOKS

(*See* Books and Documents)

DEPUTY OFFICERS

As a consequence of its general power to appoint such officers as it thinks necessary,[1] a parish council which has appointed a clerk or treasurer may appoint a standing deputy of that officer, for the purpose of acting in his place whenever the office is vacant or the holder is unable to act. A deputy thus appointed will have, subject to the terms of his appointment, all the functions of the holder of the office. The parish council may pay a deputy officer, not being a member of the council, such reasonable sum as it may determine.

Similarly, if the office of clerk or treasurer is vacant, or the holder is unable to act, and no standing deputy has been appointed or, if appointed, is unable to act, the parish council may in such case appoint a temporary deputy to act in the vacant office; and, subject to the terms of his appointment, the person so appointed will have all the functions of the holder of the office. As in the case of a standing deputy, the council may pay a person appointed as temporary deputy officer, not being a member of the council, such reasonable remuneration as it may determine.

As to disclosure by an officer of his interest in any contract, *see* "Clerk of the Parish Council".

---

[1] L.G.A. 1972, s. 112.

DESTRUCTION OF BOOKS, ETC.

(See Books and Documents)

DISCLOSURE OF INTEREST

(See Code of Conduct)

DISQUALIFICATIONS FOR OFFICE OF PARISH COUNCILLOR

(See *also* Interest in Contract or Other Matters—Parish Councillor)

A person is disqualified for being elected or being a member of a parish council if he has, within five years before his election or since his election, been convicted of crime, and has had passed upon him a sentence of imprisonment (whether suspended or not) for a period of not less than three months without the option of a fine, or has been adjudged a bankrupt, or made a composition or arrangement with his creditors; or holds any paid office or employment (other than the office of chairman or vice chairman), the appointment to which is made or confirmed by the parish council, or by any committee of the council (including a joint committee), or by any employee of the council, or is disqualified under the provisions relating to corrupt or illegal practices.[1]

In addition, an adjudication panel or a case tribunal established under Part III, Chapter IV of the Local Government Act 2000 may disqualify a councillor for up to five years for failure to comply with the council's code of conduct[2] (*see* "Code of Conduct").

---

[1] L.G.A. 1972, s. 80(1) as amended by L.G.F.A. 1982.
[2] L.G.A. 2000, s. 79.

The disqualification by reason of bankruptcy is removed and ceases if the adjudication in bankruptcy is annulled, or the bankrupt obtains his discharge. In case of composition or arrangement, the disqualification is removed on payment of his debts in full; or, in any other case, on the expiration of five years from the date on which the terms of the deed of composition or arrangement are fulfilled.[1]

A paid officer of a local authority who is employed under the direction of a committee or sub-committee, any member of which is appointed on the nomination of the parish council, is disqualified from being elected or being a member of the parish council.[2]

A person who is disqualified from being elected or being a member of the parish council is disqualified for being a member of a committee or sub-committee of the council, or for being a representative of the council on a joint committee appointed by agreement between the council and other local authorities.[3]

If a member fails throughout a period of six consecutive months from the date of his last attendance to attend any meeting of the council, he ceases to be a member of the council, unless the failure was due to some reason approved by the council *before* the expiry of that period. Approval cannot be given after the six month period has expired. Absence due to service with the Armed Forces during war or any emergency does not in any event vacate the office. Attendance at a meeting of a committee or sub-committee of the council, or at a joint committee of the council and another local authority is deemed to be attendance at a meeting of the council.[4]

---

[1] L.G.A. 1972, s. 81 as amended by the Insolvency Act 1985, Sch. 8, para. 22.
[2] L.G.A. 1972, s. 80(2).
[3] L.G.A. 1972, s. 104.
[4] L.G.A. 1972, s. 85.

Disqualifications for office of parish councillor

When a member ceases to be qualified, or becomes disqualified for any reason other than by reason of a decision by a case tribunal under s. 79 of the Local Government Act 2000, a conviction, or a breach of election laws, or ceases to be a member of the council by reason of failure to attend meetings, the council must forthwith declare the office vacant[1] and signify the vacancy by public notice. (See "Notices".)

Proceedings may be instituted, either in the High Court or in a magistrates' court, against any person acting as a member of a parish council who is disqualified from so acting.[2] Proceedings must be instituted before the expiration of six months from the date on which the person so acted. A magistrates' court can impose on the defendant to such proceedings a fine up to level 3 on the standard scale for summary offences (currently £1,000) for each occasion on which he has acted as a member of the council when disqualified. If, however, the court is satisfied that the matter would be more properly dealt with in the High Court, it must order a discontinuance of proceedings in the magistrates' court. The High Court's powers include the making of a declaration that the defendant is disqualified and that the office is vacant. An injunction may also be obtained restraining the defendant from continuing to act as if he were a member. Proceedings may not be instituted by any person other than a local government elector for the parish.

For the purposes of legal proceedings, a person is deemed to be disqualified for acting as a member of the parish council in the following cases:-

(a) if he is not qualified to be or is disqualified from being, a member of the council; or

---

[1] L.G.A. 1972, s. 86.
[2] L.G.A. 1972, s. 92.

73

(b) if, by reason of failure to make and deliver the declaration of acceptance of office within the period required, or by reason of resignation, or of failure to attend meetings of the council, he has ceased to be a member of the council.

The above provisions apply with the necessary modifications to the case of a disqualified person acting as a member of a committee or sub-committee of the parish council, or of a joint committee of which the parish council is one of the appointing authorities.

DISSOLUTION OF PARISH OR COMMUNITY COUNCIL

(See Parish Council)

DISTURBANCES AT MEETINGS

(See Meetings of Parish Council)

DITCHES AND DRAINS

(See *also* Nuisances—Sewerage)

A parish council may deal with any pond, pool, ditch, gutter or place containing, or used for the collection of, any drainage, filth, stagnant water, or matter likely to be prejudicial to health, by draining, cleansing or covering it, or otherwise preventing it from being prejudicial to health, but so as not to interfere with any private right, or with any public drainage, sewerage or sewage disposal works. Thus, for example, a parish council may clean out a village beck.

The parish council may execute any works, including works of maintenance, incidental to or consequential on any exercise of this power; and it may contribute towards the expenses incurred by any other person in doing any of the things above mentioned.[1] The council is not, however, directly empowered to take legal proceedings to enforce the abatement of any such nuisance. Where such a nuisance exists, the course to adopt is to bring the matter to the notice of the district or unitary council. If, however, the district council fails to act, the parish council has certain reserve powers (*see* "Nuisances").

At common law, there is a presumption that a roadside ditch belongs to the adjoining owner,[2] but it is a question of fact in each case. Highway authorities have the power but not a duty to clean such ditches.[3] However, the duty of highway authorities to repair and maintain highways extends to the provision of an adequate system of drainage.[4] Failure to provide this could result in an accident for which the highway authority would be liable.

DIVERSION OF A HIGHWAY

(See Highways)

DOCUMENTS

(See Books and Documents)

DRAINAGE

(See Ditches and Drains)

---

[1] P.H.A. 1936, s. 260.
[2] *Hanscombe v. Bedfordshire County Council* [1938] 3 All E.R. 647.
[3] H.A. 1980, s. 100.
[4] *Burnside v. Emerson* [1968] 1 W.L.R. 1490.

EDUCATION

For each community or voluntary school which is a primary school and which serves an area for which there is one or more "minor authorities", the governing body must include one governor appointed by that authority or those authorities.[1] A "minor authority" is, in parished areas in England, a parish council or parish meeting and, in Wales, a community council.[2] The governor need not necessarily be a parish councillor.

For secondary schools, parish councils and parish meetings have no statutory right of appointment, but the local education authority may be persuaded to provide for the parish council or meeting to nominate a governor.

ELECTION OF PARISH COUNCILLORS

(See also Disqualifications for Office of Parish Councillor—Local Government Electors—Parish Councillor—Parish Meeting)

Parish councillors are elected for a term of four years. They retire together on the fourth day after the date of the elections every four years. Their places are then filled by newly-elected councillors who come into office the same day.[3] A retiring councillor is eligible for re-election.

The term of office for a parish councillor is the same as that of the district or unitary councillor representing the same area. Consequently, in special cases where a district council changes from annual to triennial elections, or *vice versa*, the term of office of a parish councillor could, as a result, vary from the usual period.

---

[1] School Standards & Framework Act 1998, Sch. 10, para. 15.

[2] *ibid*, s. 141.

[3] L.G.A. 1972, s. 16(3) and s. 35(2).

Apart from what is stated in the Local Government Act 1972, the law relating to local council elections is now contained in the Representation of the People Acts 1983 and 1985, and local election rules made by the Home Secretary, i.e. the Local Elections (Parishes and Communities) Rules 1986 (as amended).[1]

Right to vote in local government elections depends upon the person's name having been entered in the current register of local government electors. The register is published annually not later than 1st December, following a canvas of persons in residence on 15th October. However, names may be added to or deleted from the register at any time during the year, thus creating a "rolling" register. This is intended to allow changes to be made at once, rather than on an annual basis as used to be the case. Those entitled to be registered as electors are those who are resident in the area and are British subjects,[2] citizens of the Republic of Ireland or citizens of a member state of the European Union of full age (eighteen), or who will attain full age before the end of twelve months beginning with the 1st December next, and are not subject to any legal incapacity to vote. (*See* "Local Government Electors".)

If the parish is divided into wards there will be an election of parish councillors for each ward. (*See* "Wards".) A ward must lie wholly within the area of a district or unitary council ward.

The elections are held on the first Thursday in May, unless the Secretary of State, by order made not later than the 1st February in the *preceding* year, fixes a different date.[3]

In all cases, the ordinary election of parish councillors is to be conducted by means of nomination of candidates by two electors and, if necessary, a poll.

---

[1] 1986, S.I. 2215.
[2] Which includes Commonwealth citizens.
[3] R.P.A. 1983, s. 37.

Every district or unitary council must appoint an officer of the council to be the returning officer for the election of parish councillors within the district.[1] This may be a different officer from that appointed to be the returning officer for the election of district councillors. The returning officer may delegate all or any of his functions to any person, not necessarily being an officer of the district or unitary council.[2]

The poll is to begin at eight o'clock in the morning and is to be kept open until nine o'clock in the evening.

The provisions relating to postal voting and voting by proxy have now been extended to parish council elections.[3]

Detailed rules for nomination of candidates and the conduct of an election of parish councillors will be found in the rules made by the Home Secretary referred to above, and also the forms for use thereat and the form of declaration of acceptance of office by the chairman of a parish council, and by a parish councillor. (*See* "Chairman of Parish Council" and "Parish Councillor".)

The Representation of the People Acts contain provisions relating to corrupt and illegal practices and the control of election expenses of candidates. There is a limit on expenses which is increased from time to time by Statutory Instrument. Every candidate must make a return of expenses, accompanied by a declaration in the form prescribed by the Home Secretary; this must be sent to the clerk of the district council within 28 days after the date of the election.

A candidate at an election is entitled, for the purpose of holding public meetings in furtherance of his candidature, to the use, free of charge, at reasonable times between the last day on

---

[1] R.P.A. 1983, s. 35(1).
[2] R.P.A. 1983, s. 35(4).
[3] R.P.A. 1985, s. 28 and Sch. 5.

which notice of the election may be published and the day preceding the day of election, of a suitable room in the premises of a community, foundation or voluntary school situated in the electoral area for which he is a candidate (or if there is no such school in that area, in any such school in an adjacent electoral area), or in a parish or community in part comprised in that electoral area.

He may also use any meeting room situated in the electoral area for which he is standing or in a parish or community in part comprised in that electoral area, the expense of maintaining which is payable wholly or mainly out of public funds or out of any rate, or by a body whose expenses are so payable. The school hours must not be interfered with; nor may any part of the school premises which is used as part of a private dwelling-house be used for the above purpose. Furthermore, the candidate must defray any expense incurred by reason of the use of the room for the purpose of his candidature and the cost of making good any damage caused by such use.[1]

The district or unitary council shall pay the expenses properly incurred in holding the election, not exceeding such scale as may be fixed so far as applicable. Where polls for the election of parish councillors and district or unitary councillors for the same area are taken together, one-half of the expenses is to be treated as attributable to the election of parish councillors. However, the district or unitary council may require the parish or community council to repay the election expenses it incurs.[2]

If a parish council has not been properly constituted, or becomes unable to act from failure to elect or otherwise, the district or unitary council may order a new election to be held and may, by order, make provision for authorising any person

---

[1] R.P.A. 1983, s. 96, as substituted by R.P.A. 1985, Sch. 4, para. 38.
[2] R.P.A. 1983, s. 36(5), as amended by the Local Government Finance (Repeals and Consequential Amendments) Order 1991.

to act temporarily in the place of the parish council and of the chairman of the parish council. They are empowered for the above purpose to do anything which is deemed necessary or expedient for carrying the order into effect.[1]

In the event of a casual vacancy upon a parish council by death or disqualification or in any other way, the vacancy must be publicly notified and a by-election conducted in accordance with the rules for ordinary elections if within 14 days a poll is claimed by ten electors.[2] Otherwise, it is to be filled by co-option as soon as practicable and the council must be convened forthwith to fill the vacancy if the period of vacancy has six months or more to run. If the period is less than six months, the council may still fill the vacancy by co-option if it so chooses but it is not obliged to do so.[3] The person filling a casual vacancy retires from office at the time when the councillor whose place he has filled would ordinarily have retired.[4]

If there is more than one candidate for co-option, the council must vote, if necessary by successive counts which eliminate the least successful candidate, until the successful candidate receives an *absolute* majority of those present at the council meeting and voting.

If the membership of a parish council has been increased during the term of office of the existing members, the vacancies are not casual and must be filled by a by-election.

ELECTORS

(See Local Government Electors)

---

[1] R.P.A. 1983, s. 39(4).
[2] Local Elections (Parish and Communities) Rules 1986, S.I. 2215.
[3] L.G.A. 1972, s. 89(6), and Local Elections (Parishes and Communities) Rules 1986, S.I. 2215, rule 8.
[4] L.G.A. 1972, s. 90.

ELIGIBILITY FOR OFFICE

(See Parish Councillor)

EMPLOYEES

(See *also* Agency—Clerk of Parish Council—Deputy Officers—Gratuities to Officers—Superannuation of Paid Officers—Treasurer of Parish Council)

A parish council has a general power to employ any persons it considers necessary for the proper discharge of its functions.[1] If the function is one which the parish council does not have a statutory power to perform but is covered by the free resource, the cost must be borne by this fund[2] (*see* "Free Resource"). An example is the employment of a village sweeper. Every appointment of a paid officer or employee must be made on merit.[3]

In the case of any paid employee, including the clerk, the council has certain obligations. These include the deduction and payment to the Inland Revenue of income tax and the payment of National Insurance contributions as appropriate.

Fidelity security is essential (*see* "Insurance").

All employees have extensive rights under employment rights legislation, including the right to be provided with a written statement of the employer's terms and conditions of service.[4]

All employees in Wales are subject to a code of conduct issued by the National Assembly.[5] The code came into force on 28th

---

[1] L.G.A. 1972, s. 112.
[2] L.G.A. 1972, s. 137.
[3] L.G.H.A. 1989, s. 7.
[4] Employment Rights Act 1996, s. 1.
[5] Code of Conduct (Qualifying Local Government Employees) (Wales) Order 2001 (S.I. 2280 (W.170)).

81

July 2001. A similar code will be promulgated by the Secretary of State in England. At the time of writing (April 2003), consultations on the proposed code were taking place. It is likely that the code will be published before the end of 2003 and will not differ markedly from the Welsh code.

Care must be taken to comply with the statutory obligations to ensure the health and safety of employees.[1]

Insurance in respect of the council's liability against injury sustained by an employee during the course of his employment is *compulsory*, whether the employee is part time or full time.[2]

Any council faced with a claim for unfair dismissal or sex, race or disability discrimination should seek legal advice, as each case tends to turn on its own facts and the financial consequences to the council may be considerable.

ENTERTAINMENT AND THE ARTS

(*See also* Tourism)

A parish council has the power to provide entertainments of any nature or facilities for dancing.[3] It can provide a theatre, a concert hall, a dance hall or any other premises suitable for entertainments. It can spend money on maintaining a band or orchestra. It may do anything which furthers the development of the arts and local crafts. A parish council may set apart any part of its parks or pleasure grounds for any of these purposes subject to any covenant. It can also contribute to the expenses of any other local authority or anyone who is providing any of these facilities.

---

[1] Health and Safety at Work Act 1974.
[2] Employers Liability (Compulsory Insurance) Act 1969.
[3] L.G.A. 1972, s. 145.

EXPENSES AND EXPENDITURE

(*See also* **Allowances to Parish Councillors—Loans to Parish Council**)

A parish council is empowered to incur expenditure in the execution of any works, including works of maintenance or improvement, or on anything which is calculated to facilitate, or is conducive or incidental to, the exercise of its statutory powers[1] (all of which are indicated under their appropriate headings in this book) or in relation to any parish property. There is also a power to incur expenditure for the benefit of the area for all or some of its inhabitants.[2] (*See* "Free Resource".)

With the exception of expenditure under the "free resource", all rate limits have now been abolished.[3]

The expenses of a parish council are chargeable separately on the parish and the council obtains funds for the purpose of defraying these expenses by means of precepts issued to the council responsible for collecting local government taxes.[4] A parish council is a local precepting authority and may issue a precept for each financial year before 1st March in the preceding financial year (although it is not invalid merely because it is issued on or after that date).[5] It is important for councils to prepare accurate budgets in order to ensure that they will receive the monies during the year which are necessary for the proper carrying out of the council's functions. The council responsible for the collection of local government taxes cannot challenge the amount of the precept. It is inadvisable for a parish council to make any arrangement with that council

---

[1] L.G.A. 1972, s. 111.
[2] L.G.A. 1972, s. 137.
[3] L.G.A. 1972, s. 30.
[4] i.e. the district or unitary council. L.G.A. 1972, s. 150.
[5] L.G.F.A. 1992, s. 41.

which interferes with its right to precept. If there is a separate council, the expenses of the parish meeting are paid by the parish council. These expenses will form part of the ordinary expenses of the parish council.

The expenses of a district or unitary council are normally charged as general expenses on the whole of the district or county but a district or unitary council must charge as special expenses on a parish any expenses incurred in the parish by performing therein any function performed elsewhere in the district or county by a parish council, unless it passes a resolution to treat them as general expenses.[1]

Every cheque or other order for payment of money by a parish council must be signed by two members of the council. (*See* "Accounts".) This is a responsible duty, and every signatory must ensure that payments are made only in accordance with the decisions of the council.

Where there is no parish council, a parish meeting in England meets its own expenses, usually by precepting on the district or unitary council. In Wales, the expenses of a community meeting where there is no community council are met by the county or county borough council.

For the tax position of parish councils, *see* "Income Tax" and "Value Added Tax".

FIDELITY SECURITY

(See Insurance—Treasurer of Parish Council)

FIELD GARDENS

(See Allotments)

---

[1] L.G.F.A. 1992, s. 35.

FINANCE

**(See Accounts—Allowances to Parish Councillors—
Audit—Expenses and Expenditure—Free Resource—
Funds and Accumulations—Income Tax—Investment —
Loans to Parish Council—Rating and Valuation—
Subscriptions to Associations—Value Added Tax)**

FINANCIAL STATEMENT OF PARISH COUNCIL

(See Accounts—Audit)

FLAGPOLES

A parish council may with the consent of the highway authority erect flagpoles on any highway in its own area and may make slots in the highway for them.

The parish council must ensure that the apparatus causes as little obstruction to the highway or interference with the enjoyment of adjacent premises as possible, does not interfere with traffic signs, and is properly maintained and (if necessary to prevent danger) lit.[1]

FOOTPATHS

(See *also* Footways—Highways)

A public footpath is a highway over which the public have a right of way on foot only, other than a path at the side of a public road.[2] The latter are usually known as footways. (*See* "Footways".) A public bridleway is a footpath with additional rights, i.e. to ride or lead a horse.

---

[1] H.A. 1980, s. 144.
[2] H.A. 1980, s. 30.

A parish council may create a public footpath (or any highway) by means of an agreement with the landowner.[1] In addition, the parish council may undertake the repair and maintenance of all or any of the public footpaths or bridleways within its parish. The exercise of this power will not relieve any other authority or person from any liability with respect to repair or maintenance of a public footpath. In particular, the county council must maintain all paths in existence in December 1949.[2] For the *standard* of repair, *see* "Highways". It is entirely optional whether a parish council undertakes the repair of any public footpath. It cannot be compelled to do so. If the parish council resolves to repair, it should inform the county council, as the highway authority in all parishes. The county council may in such cases meet the whole or part of the expenditure the parish council incurs.

For obstruction of footpaths generally, *see* "Highways". A parish council has no power to compel an owner to cut back hedges but the county council or district council may so order the owner to do this at the request of the parish council if it is necessary to keep the footpaths safe and fit for normal use.[3]

A landowner has a legal duty to keep gates and stiles safe and to the standard of repair necessary to prevent unreasonable interference with users, but the landowner may claim a quarter of his expenses from the highway authority. If he fails in his duty, the highway authority may do the work at his expense after 14 days' notice.[4]

Driving a motor vehicle or riding a motor-cycle on a footpath or bridleway is an offence. However, restrictions on the use of vehicles on footpaths, footways or bridleways do not affect

---

[1] H.A. 1980, s. 43.
[2] H.A. 1980, s. 36.
[3] H.A. 1980, s. 154.
[4] H.A. 1980, s. 146.

the use by the parish council of vehicles or equipment for the maintenance of the way within certain prescribed limits.[1] It is not a criminal offence to ride a horse on a footpath (although it is on a footway), unless there is a by-law in force to this effect.

There is no obligation on a parish council to fence a footpath or to maintain an existing fence. If, however, the council removes and fails to replace a fence erected by it or its predecessors to guard a dangerous place, the council may be liable under the law of tort in respect of any accident resulting therefrom.

Where a public path crosses agricultural land, or land which is being brought into use for agriculture, and it is convenient and in accordance with the rules of good husbandry to plough the path in ploughing the land, the farmer may do so. This does not, however, apply to a path at the side of a field. After the ploughing is completed, if the disturbance to the surface is for sowing a crop, he must make good the surface of the path for the exercise of the public right of way not later than two weeks from the time when he *began* to plough the path. This period may be extended, on application, for a further period not exceeding 28 days. Failure to restore within the time limits renders him liable to a fine at level 3 on the standard scale for summary offences (currently £1,000).[2] A farmer who ploughs any path otherwise than in exercise of the above right to plough is guilty of an offence and subject to a fine at level 3 on the standard scale (currently £1,000). A prosecution can be brought by the highway authority or by the parish council.

The Highways Act 1980 has been further amended in respect of disturbance to footpaths and bridleways by the Rights of Way Act 1990.

---

[1] R.T.A. 1988, s. 34; H.A. 1980, s. 300.
[2] H.A. 1980, s. 134 as amended and substituted by the Rights of Way Act 1990.

If it is represented to the highway authority that for agricultural purposes it is expedient that stiles, gates or other works for preventing the ingress or egress of animals should be erected on a public footpath crossing the land, the highway authority may authorise their erection subject to such condition as they may impose for maintenance and for enabling the right of way to be exercised without undue inconvenience to the public.[1]

A parish council has power to erect direction posts on public paths with the consent of the county council. Such posts may also be erected by the county council, as highway authority. The county council has a *duty* to erect signposts at every point where a footpath or bridleway or a byway open to all traffic leaves a metal road, unless the parish council agrees with the county council that a sign is not necessary.[2] Parish councils should ensure that the county councils comply with this statutory duty.

It is an offence on or near any way shown on the definitive map to put a notice containing any false or misleading statement likely to deter the public from using the way.[3] It is the duty of the highway authority to enforce this provision, and they or the district or unitary council[4] can bring proceedings for this purpose.

It is unlawful for a bull to be at large in a field through which there is a footpath unless it does not exceed the age of ten months or, not being of a recognised dairy breed, it is at large with cows or heifers in the same field.[5] A recognised dairy

---

[1] H.A. 1980, s. 147.
[2] C.A. 1968, s. 27 as amended by the Wildlife and Countryside Act 1981, s.65.
[3] N.P.A. 1949, s. 57.
[4] L.G.A. 1972, Sch. 21, para. 97.
[5] Wildlife and Countryside Act 1981, s. 59.

breed means one of the following: Ayrshire, British Friesian, British Holstein, Dairy Shorthorn, Guernsey, Jersey or Kerry.

Any question of the improper use of the highway, e.g. the use of a footpath by cycles or other vehicles, is not directly a matter for the parish council but for the highway authority. As a result of the Countryside Act 1968, a cycle may now legally be ridden on a bridleway.[1]

The use of a footpath includes the use of prams and push-chairs as a reasonable accompaniment of a pedestrian.[2] It has never been decided by the courts whether a dog is a reasonable accompaniment of a pedestrian, although it is usually assumed that this is so. However, just like the pedestrian, if the dog strays from the footpath, there is technically a trespass. In practice this can only be avoided by keeping the dog on a lead.

FOOTWAYS

A footway is a footpath at the side of a public road. It is part of the highway and is maintainable by the highway authority. A highway authority has a duty to provide a footway in any case where it considers that the provision of such a footway is necessary or desirable for the safety or accommodation of pedestrians.[3]

The law relating to footpaths (*see* "Footpaths") does not, in general terms, apply to footways. Thus, a parish council has no specific power to maintain a footway.

A parish council may provide seats and shelters on a footway (*see* "Roadside Seats and Shelters" and "Bus Shelters"). For footway lighting, *see* "Lighting".

---

[1] C.A. 1968, s. 30.
[2] *R. v. Mathias* (1861) 2 F. & F. 570.
[3] H.A. 1980, s. 54.

FREE RESOURCE

The Local Government (Financial Provisions) Act 1963 first gave parish councils this very useful general power in what came to be known as the free fifth. Subsequently, it was extended by the 1972 Act into the free twopence and, consequent upon changes in the rating system, it is now usual to refer to it as the "free resource".[1] Under it, a parish council may spend every year up to a specified limit on anything which in the opinion of the parish council is in the interests of the parish, or any part of it, or is in the interests of all or some of its inhabitants. Examples include Armistice Day wreaths, employment of village sweeper, presentation to retiring member, etc. It may also be used to make contributions to any charitable body or any body providing a public service otherwise than for gain, anywhere in the United Kingdom, or to any appeal fund devised in connection with a particular event in the United Kingdom by the Lord Mayor of London or the Chairman of a county or district council. For the use of the free resource in connection with land acquired for the benefit of the area, *see* "Property of Parish Council".

These terms are very wide and the reference to "the council's opinion" ensures that, provided the council do not act quite unreasonably, their discretion is not open to challenge.

The power is, however, subject to the limitation that it may not be used where some other power, whether conditional or unconditional, is available. This means that the power cannot be used to circumvent a requirement for Ministerial consent, or to evade some restriction on the amount which can be spent for a certain purpose.

---

[1] L.G.A. 1972, s. 137, as amended. The amount is currently £3.50 per elector on the electoral roll on 1st April in England and £5.00 per elector in Wales. Under the Local Government Bill currently before Parliament (April 2003), the amount in England will be raised to £5.00 and, in both countries, further increases will be linked automatically to the movement of retail prices.

It is important that the expenditure be authorised in advance by a formal resolution of the council. This is because such expenditure should be shown in a separate account, which is to be open to inspection by a local government elector in the same way as is the council's accounts (*see* "Inspection of Documents").

FREEDOM OF INFORMATION

Under the Freedom of Information Act 2000, all local authorities, including parish councils, and parish meetings in England where there is no council, must make available to the public certain types of information. In particular, they must adopt and maintain a publication scheme showing the information they provide and how it can be inspected.[1] Each scheme must be approved by the Information Commissioner, who may issue model schemes.[2] A model scheme for local councils has been published and can be viewed on the Commissioner's website (www. informationcommissioner.gov.uk).

All councils were obliged to adopt a publication scheme before the end of 2002 and to activate it before the end of February 2003.

Most of the information required to be published under the 2000 Act is already covered by other legislation (see "Inspection of Documents").

FUEL ALLOTMENTS

(See Allotments)

---

[1] Freedom of Information Act 2000, s. 19.
[2] *ibid*., s. 20.

FUND RAISING

(See Income)

FUNDS AND ACCUMULATIONS

A parish council has power to set up a loans fund for debt repayment,[1] and such other funds, other than a superannuation fund, as it thinks fit.[2] It may pay into such funds such sums as it thinks fit. Thus a parish council may provide for the renewal and repair of any of its assets. In respect of the application of capital money on disposal of land, the consent of the Secretary of State is required under s. 153 of the Local Government Act 1972. A general disposal consent has been issued by him and may be viewed on the O.D.P.M. website (www.odpm.gov.uk).

Pending the application of the funds for their respective purposes, the money in the fund should be invested in statutory securities. (*See* "Investment".)

GIFTS OF PROPERTY

(See Bus Shelters—Property of Parish Council—War Memorials)

GRANTS

A parish council may be able to obtain a grant from several sources. A county council may make a grant to a parish council, or a parish meeting in England without a council, towards expenditure relating to public open spaces.[3] The National

---

[1] L.G.A. 1972, Sch. 13—funds of local authorities, para. 15.

[2] L.G.(M.P.)A. 1976, s. 28.

[3] L.G.A. 1958, s. 56.

Playing Fields Association, 25A Ovington Square, London, SW3 1LQ may provide a grant for the provision of playing fields and equipment. Grants for sports provision may also be available from, or through, Sport England, 16 Upper Woburn Place, London, WC1H 0QP or the Sports Council for Wales, Sophia Gardens, Cardiff, CF1 9SW. The Countryside Agency, John Dower House, Crescent Place, Cheltenham, Glos, GL50 3RA has power to grant-aid expenditure for the conservation and enhancement of the natural beauty and amenity of the countryside or for the provision of facilities for the enjoyment of the countryside.[1] D.E.F.R.A. may give grants for broadly the same purposes under the Countryside Stewardship scheme.[2] A highway authority or a district council may contribute to expenditure by a parish council on footpath or bridleway maintenance.[3]

The Secretary of State may grant-aid any body which encourages the public not to deface places by litter and a county council or a district council may contribute towards the provision by a parish council of litter bins.[4] The Secretary of State may give grants for the reclaiming or improvement of derelict land.[5] A.C.R.E. (Action for Communities in Rural England), Somerford Court, Somerford Road, Cirencester, Glos, GL7 1TW administers grant funds for village halls and for rural improvement projects in England. In Wales, grants may be available for environmental projects from the Countryside Council for Wales, Maes y Ffynnon, Penrhosgarnedd, Bangor, Gwynedd, LL57 2DN. Parish councils may be able to obtain grants from the National Heritage Memorial Fund and the other National Lottery funds. Some principal councils make concurrent function grants to

---

[1] N.P.A. 1949, s. 1; C.A. 1968, s. 1.
[2] Environment Act 1998, s. 98.
[3] H.A. 1980, s. 43(2).
[4] Litter Act 1983, ss. 3 and 6.
[5] Derelict Land Act 1982, s. 1.

parish councils to cover the whole, or part, of the expenditure by a parish council on a concurrent function which is exercised by the principal council as well.

GRATUITIES TO OFFICERS

The general effect of case law is that remuneration must be related to the current responsibilities of the office and any gratuity not so related is ordinarily illegal.

Gratuities may, however, be payable upon retirement, *see* "Superannuation of Paid Officers".

GRAVES

(See Burial and Cremation)

GREENS

(See Village Greens)

GROUPING OF PARISHES

England

A parish may be grouped under an order of the district or unitary council with some neighbouring (not necessarily adjoining) parish or parishes under a common parish council.[1] In such cases, however, there must be a separate parish meeting for every parish so grouped. Each parish must be separately represented on the parish council for the group. The grouping may be dissolved upon application to the above principal council by the council of the grouped parishes or of the parish meeting for any one of the grouped parishes.

---

[1] L.G.A. 1972, ss. 11 and 29.

Grouping of parishes

The parish meeting of any parish may apply to the above principal council for a voluntary grouping order. The consent of the parish meetings of the other parishes proposed to be grouped is essential.

Where a grouping order is in force, it provides for preserving the separate rights of each parish as to appointments of trustees and beneficiaries of charities and the custody of documents, and may provide for the consent of a particular parish meeting to any particular act of the council.

The rule that, in England, the number of councillors on a parish council must not be less than five[1] does not mean that there must be at least five councillors for each parish in the group. The number from each parish can be less.

Wales

A community meeting may apply to the county or county borough council for an order grouping the community with some neighbouring community or communities under a common community council, or for adding the community to an existing common community council. However, an application may only be made if (a) a poll of local government electors for the community has been held, (b) a majority of those voting in the poll supports the application, and (c) the application is made jointly with the communities to be grouped. The decision to hold a poll must be made at a community meeting at which at least 30% of the electorate or, if that number exceeds 300, at least 300, electors are present. At least 30 clear days' notice of the meeting must be given.

A similar procedure applies where the dissolution of a common community council is sought.

[1] L.G.A. 1972, s. 16(1).

If a proposal to form or dissolve a common community council is rejected in a poll, a further poll cannot be held for at least two years. Furthermore, such a proposal cannot be made for two years after changes made following a review by the Local Government Boundary Commission for Wales or following a successful application for a grouping/dissolution order.[1]

GUARANTEE POLICY

(See Insurance—Treasurer of Parish Council)

HACKNEY CARRIAGE

(See Licences)

HALLS

(See Village Halls)

HERBAGE

(See Roadside Wastes)

HIGHWAYS

(See *also* Flagpoles—Footpaths—Roadside Wastes)

The county council, metropolitan district council or unitary council (in Wales, the county or county borough council) is the local highway authority for all highways in a parish, although the district council may have certain powers.[2]

---

[1] L.G.A. 1972, ss. 28-30.
[2] H.A. 1980, s. 1(2).

The word "highway" includes all defined routes (e.g. roads, bridges, carriageways, cartways, horseways, footpaths, bridleways, footways, causeways, churchways and pavements) over which members of the public may lawfully pass. The highway authority will be responsible for the maintenance of most of these to the standard required by law, i.e. to be reasonably passable for the ordinary traffic of the neighbourhood for all seasons of the year.[1] The duty to repair can be enforced if necessary by following the procedure laid down in the Highways Act 1980.[2]

Is there a right of way?

Where a way over any land has been actually enjoyed by the public as of right and without interruption for 20 years, it shall be deemed to have been dedicated as a highway, unless there is sufficient evidence that there was no intention during that period to dedicate.[3] A right of way over land does not include a public right of navigation over a river.[4]

An owner of land (or the reversioner, where the land is let or leased) over which a way used by the public passes may place a notice on the land indicating that the way is not dedicated as a highway. Any such notice, placed in such a manner as to be visible to those using the way, shall, in the absence of proof of a contrary intention, be sufficient evidence to negate the intention of the owner to dedicate the way as a highway.[5]

However, if no such notice has been displayed, or it has been torn down or defaced, notice in writing sent by the owner of the land to the council of the county and to the council of the district in which the way is situate stating that the way is not

---

[1] *R. v. High Halden* (1859) 1 F. & F. 678.

[2] H.A. 1980, s. 56.

[3] H.A. 1980, s. 31. *Gloucestershire C.C. v. Farrow* (1983) 2 All E.R. 1031.

[4] *Yorkshire Derwent Trust Ltd. v. Brotherton* [1989] 2 All E.R. 423.

[5] H.A. 1980, s. 31(3).

dedicated, shall, in the absence of proof of a contrary intention, be sufficient evidence to negate the intention of the owner to dedicate the way as a highway.[1]

The owner of any land may deposit at any time with the council of the county and with the council of the district in which the land is situate, a map on a scale of not less than six inches to the mile, delineating his land, together with a statement indicating what ways he admits have been dedicated as highways.[2]

The Act does not require these maps and statements to be deposited with parish councils, but parish councils should, nevertheless, take steps to inspect them, so that they may be in a position to make representations to the district council regarding any public rights of way not shown on any such maps or indicated in the statement accompanying the map.

Any court or other tribunal, before determining whether a way has been dedicated as a highway, or the date upon which dedication, if any, took place, shall take into consideration "any map, plan or history of the locality, or other relevant document tendered in evidence", and that such weight shall be given thereto as the court or tribunal considers justified by the circumstances.

Definitive maps and statements

Most rights of way in England and Wales are shown on maps prepared and kept up to date by surveying authorities (county councils, metropolitan district councils and unitary councils in England; county and county borough councils in Wales). Depiction of a path or way on the definitive map is conclusive evidence that there is a public right of way. There is a fairly

---

[1] H.A. 1980, s. 31(5).
[2] H.A. 1980, s. 31(6).

elaborate procedure for altering the definitive map where a change in the path network takes place. Parish councils have a right to be consulted about, and to be notified of, any proposed changes.

The definitive map is accompanied by a definitive statement. This describes the route of each path and any limitations or conditions, both legal and physical, to which the path may be subject. In practice, most definitive statements simply describe briefly the route of a path.

The principal legislation covering definitive maps is the National Parks and Access to the Countryside Act 1949 and the Wildlife and Countryside Act 1981.

Acquisition and agreements

Where the parish council is satisfied that the dedication of a highway will be for the benefit of the inhabitants of the parish, or of any part thereof, it may enter into an agreement with any person having the necessary power for the dedication by that person of a highway over land in the parish or any adjoining parish.[1] Any right of way so acquired would necessarily be a public highway dedicated to general public use.

A parish council may also acquire by agreement a right of way which is *not* a public highway, e.g. one restricted to the inhabitants of the parish or any part thereof.[2]

The parish council may carry out any maintenance or improvement work to any such highway or right of way. It may be noted that the above powers are not limited to footpaths, but include carriageways.

---

[1] H.A. 1980, s. 30.
[2] L.G.A. 1894, s. 8.

The district council, with the consent of the highway authority and the local planning authority, may also acquire rights of way both by agreement and compulsorily.

Obstructions

If a parish council considers that any highway has been unlawfully stopped up or obstructed, it may make representation to that effect to the county council which then has a *duty* to take proceedings to remove the obstruction, unless satisfied that the allegations are incorrect.[1] The fact that the highway is not on the definitive map does not preclude the county council from taking action if there is clear evidence of the existence of the public right of way.[2]

The special needs of disabled or blind persons in respect of obstacles on the highway must be considered by the highway authority.[3]

(For encroachment on roadside wastes forming part of the highway—*see* "Roadside Wastes".)

Provision of trees and verges

The parish council may, with the consent of the highway authority, plant trees, shrubs and other plants and lay out grass verges in a highway maintainable at the public expense.[4] The power includes a power to do anything expedient for the maintenance or protection of anything provided by them or anyone else, including the provision (and subsequent removal) of guards or fences to protect the plantings. As a result of private Acts, parish councils in some counties may carry out such work without the consent of the highway authority.

---

[1] H.A. 1980, s. 130.

[2] *R. v. Ogden* [1963] 1 All E.R. 574.

[3] H.A. 1980, s. 175A, inserted by the Disabled Persons Act 1981.

[4] H.A. 1980, s. 116.

Stopping up, or diversion, of a highway or public path

In the case of a highway other than a trunk or special road, a highway authority may apply to the magistrates' court for authority to stop it up or divert it on the ground that is is unnecessary[1] or that a diversion will make it nearer or more commodious to the public.[2] If the highway is a classified road, the parish council or, in England if none, the chairman of the parish meeting must, amongst others, be given at least 28 days' notice and is entitled to appear before the magistrates' court and be heard. Any other person likely to be aggrieved may also be heard and this presumably includes a parish council of a neighbouring parish. If, however, the highway is an unclassified road, the highway authority must give notice that it proposes to make the application to both the district council and the parish council or, in England where there is no parish council, to the Chairman of the parish meeting, and if within two months any of these give notice to the highway authority that they have refused their consent, the highway authority may not make the application at all.

Any two magistrates of the court may view the highway in question. The court cannot authorise a diversion without the written consent of all those with legal interests in the land over which the diversion is to be made, and an order can reserve a footway or bridleway.

Whilst the magistrates' court procedure is only available to highway authorities and applies, apart from trunk and special roads, to all highways including footpaths and bridleways, a county council or a district council has a special procedure available to it for extinguishing by order a public right of way over any footpath or bridleway in its area.[3] The council can

---

[1] For the meaning of unnecessary see *Ramblers Association v. Kent* C.C. [1990] 60 Planning and Compensation Reports, 464.

[2] H.A. 1980, s. 96.

[3] H.A. 1980, s. 118; Public Path Orders Regulations 1993 (S.I. 9).

make such an order (called a public path extinguishment order) *only on the ground that the path or way is not needed for public use.* If the order is opposed it must be confirmed by the Secretary of State and, before it is submitted to him for confirmation, the council must give at least 28 days' notice in the London Gazette, a local newspaper and to the parish council or parish meeting, and must post a notice near the land concerned. If objections are made, the Secretary of State holds a public inquiry. He is bound to hold such an inquiry if the objector is a local authority (including a parish council, or parish meeting if there is no parish council). If the order is not opposed, the district council may confirm the order themselves.

A county council or district council also has a power to make a similar order for diversion of a footpath or bridleway (called a public path diversion order), where it appears to the council that, in the interests of the owner or occupier of the land crossed by the path or way, it is expedient to divert it.[1] There is provision in respect of confirmation by the Secretary of State if the order is opposed, with the important provision that the Secretary of State must then be satisfied that the diverted path will not be substantially less convenient to the public.

Other provisions relating to stopping up or diverting highways are as follows. A housing authority may extinguish rights of way over land purchased for slum clearance and redevelopment. Similar provision is made for the extinguishment of public rights of way over land acquired or appropriated for planning purposes by a local authority if that authority is satisfied that an alternative right of way

---

[1] H.A. 1980, s. 119, as amended by the Wildlife and Countryside Act 1981, Sch. 16, para. 5. For the procedure for making such orders see the Highways Act 1980, Sch. 6, as amended by the Wildlife and Countryside Act 1981, Sch. 16. See also the Public Path Orders Regulations 1993 (S.I. 9).

has been or will be provided, or is not required in the circumstances.

The Acquisition of Land Act 1981 confers a general power if land is purchased, whether compulsorily or by agreement where a power of compulsory acquisition could have been used, to stop up public rights of way other than those enjoyed by vehicular traffic, subject to the Secretary of State being satisfied that an alternative right of way has been or will be provided, or is not required in the circumstances.[1]

There is also a provision in the Town and Country Planning Act 1990 for the stopping up or diversion of highways (including footpaths or bridleways) by order of the Secretary of State if he is satisfied that it is necessary to do so in order to enable development to be carried out in accordance with a planning permission or in certain other circumstances.[2] The county council, or district council exercising planning powers, now has similar powers, subject to confirmation by the Secretary of State.[3]

The Secretary of State may, in connection with the construction or improvement of a highway, make an order diverting or stopping up any other highway if it appears to him to be expedient to do so, in the interests of the safety of users of the main highway or to facilitate the movement of traffic on the main highway.

A highway over which the public has a right of way with vehicles (not being a trunk road or other main road) may be converted by Ministerial Order to a footpath or bridleway if a resolution by the local planning authority for improving the

---

[1] Acquisition of Land Act 1981, s. 32.
[2] T.C.P.A. 1990, s. 247.
[3] T.C.P.A. 1990, s. 259; Town and Country Planning (Public Path Orders) Regulations 1993 (S.I. 10).

amenity of their area includes a proposal to convert a highway in that manner.

Signs

A parish council may put up a village name sign,[1] a bus stop, or a warning sign on a public highway, other than a footpath or bridleway, with the permission of the local highway authority. It may also provide warning signs on footpaths or bridleways without such permission.[2] (For direction signs on footpaths, *see* "Footpaths.")

Control of roadside sales

Sales from stalls on vehicles which are stationed either on a verge or a layby or on any unenclosed land within 15 metres of the road are unlawful if their presence causes, or is likely to cause, danger on the road or interrupts, or is likely to interrupt, any user of the road.[3]

Traffic calming

A parish council may contribute towards the cost of traffic calming measures (e.g. road humps) provided by a highway authority if the council thinks they will be of benefit to its area.[4]

HIRING OF LAND

(See Allotments—Property of Parish Council)

HOUSE TO HOUSE COLLECTIONS

(See Income)

---

[1] Which may include a crest, with the Secretary of State's permission.
[2] R.T.R.A. 1984, s. 72.
[3] H.A. 1980, s. 147A, inserted by L.G.(M.P.)A. 1982, s. 23.
[4] H.A. 1980, s. 274A, inserted by L.G.R.A. 1997, s. 30.

HOUSING

Parish councils have no statutory functions in regard to the provision of housing. There seems no reason, however, why a parish council should not acquire land by agreement to make this available for a housing association if in the council's opinion this would be for the benefit of the parish.[1]

A parish council may complain to the officer of the council responsible for public health in writing that any house is unfit for human habitation or that any area should be dealt with as a clearance area, whereupon that officer has a duty to inspect the house or the area and to report to the housing authority stating the facts and whether, in his opinion, the house is unfit or the area should be so treated.[2]

INCLOSURE OF COMMONS

(See Commons)

INCOME

(See *also* Expenses—Lotteries)

A parish council obtains most of its income for its own revenue purposes through precepts to the council responsible for the collection of local government taxes,[3] but may also have, or utilise, a number of other sources, e.g. income from letting property; income from investments and bank deposits; income from public subscriptions, whist drives, etc. House to house collections require a licence from the council responsible for the collection of local government taxes, unless the purpose

---

[1] L.G.A. 1972, s. 124.

[2] Housing Act 1985, s. 606(2) as amended.

[3] L.G.F.A. 1992, s. 41.

of the collection is purely local in character and a certificate of exemption is obtained from the Chief Constable.[1]

INCOME TAX

(*See also* Value Added Tax)

Parish councils are not liable for income tax on their income, nor for corporation tax or capital gains tax.[2]

INCORPORATION OF PARISH COUNCIL

(See Parish Council)

INFORMATION ABOUT LAND

A parish council requiring information about the ownership or occupation of land with a view to exercising any of its statutory functions, may serve a notice on the occupier, freeholder, leaseholder, mortgagee, any person receiving rent, or any person authorised to manage or let the land. The notice must specify the land and the statutory function and may require the person served to advise the council of the nature of his own interest and the name and address of the occupier and every person believed by him to fall into one of the above categories.[3]

If the land has registered title, this procedure may not be necessary because the Register is open to public inspection.

---

[1] House to House Collections Act 1939, s. 1.
[2] Income and Corporation Taxes Act 1988, s. 519 and Taxation of Chargeable Gains Act 1992, s. 271.
[3] L.G.(M.P.)A. 1976, s. 16, as amended.

INFORMATION FOR THE PUBLIC

(*See also* Freedom of Information)

A parish council may make arrangements, or assist in the
making of arrangements, whereby the public may readily obtain
on application information on services provided by *any* local
authority, government department, charity or voluntary
organisation, or any other information relating to the functions
of the parish council.[1] A parish council may, in connection
with the provision of information on the functions of the parish
council, arrange for publications, lectures, films, exhibitions,
etc., or contribute towards the cost of preparing these.

INQUIRIES

(See Public Inquiries)

INSPECTION OF DOCUMENTS

(*See also* Books and Documents—Freedom of Information)

In general terms, any requirement that a parish council shall
keep a document of any description is satisfied if it keeps a
photographic copy of the document.[2]

The minutes of proceedings of the parish council must be
open to the inspection, at all reasonable hours, of any local
government elector for the parish, and he may make a copy
of, or an extract from, such minutes.[3] No payment may be
required.[4] There is no obligation to supply a copy to an elector.[5]

---

[1] L.G.A. 1972, s. 142 as amended by L.G.A. 1986, s. 3.
[2] L.G.A. 1972, s. 229.
[3] L.G.A. 1972, s. 228(1).
[4] L.G.A. 1972, s. 228(6).
[5] *Russell-Walker v Gimblett*, Chichester Crown Court, 30 March 1984.

These provisions also apply to the minutes of a committee where they are submitted to the council and so become, in effect, part of the council's minutes, but not otherwise. An elector may also inspect and make a copy of, or extract from, an order for payment of money made by the parish council.[1]

The accounts of the parish council and of its treasurer shall be open to the inspection of any member of the council, at all reasonable hours, without payment, and any such member may make a copy of, or extract from, the accounts.[2]

At the audit, the accounts, together with all books and documents relating thereto, may be inspected by any persons interested. Any such person is at liberty to make copies of, or extracts from, the deposited accounts and documents without payment.[3] The auditor must also give to any local government elector for the area, who so requests, an opportunity for that elector, or his representative, to question the auditor about the accounts.[4]

Any report by an auditor on the accounts must accompany the agenda for the meeting at which the parish council consider the report, and must not be excluded from material provided to the press.[5]

Any person having the custody of any of the above documents, who obstructs any person entitled to inspect or make a copy of, or extracts from, them is liable, on summary conviction, to a fine not exceeding level 1 on the standard scale for summary offences (currently £200).[6]

---

[1] L.G.A. 1972, s. 228(2).
[2] L.G.A. 1972, s. 228(3).
[3] A.C.A. 1998, s. 15(1).
[4] A.C.A. 1998, s. 15(2).
[5] A.C.A. 1998, s. 10.
[6] L.G.A. 1972, s. 228(7) as amended.

INSPECTION OF PARISH PROPERTY

It is a useful practice for parish councils to arrange periodic inspections of property and equipment. An up-to-date inspection book in the form of a summarised inventory with columns for each inspection is useful. Some parish councils make such inspections the duty of the vice-chairman.

INSURANCE

The importance of adequate insurance of parish councils against third party risks was underlined by a case in which a boy was awarded heavy damages in respect of injury sustained while playing in a playground belonging to the council.[1] Similar liability may arise in many ways in connection with a parish council's various functions, and it may be advisable to cover all such risks by a single public liability policy. Cover up to at least £5 million should be taken.

Care should be taken to see the buildings and other property of the council are sufficiently insured against fire and other risks. The cover should extend to the current cost of replacing the building, for which purpose annual valuations may be necessary.

Fidelity security is required to be taken by the council in respect of the treasurer.[2] Similar security is desirable in respect of other officers. This is usually done by way of a fidelity guarantee policy.

A parish council must insure against employers' liability claims.[3] (*See* "Employees".)

---

[1] *Bates v. Stone Parish Council* [1954] 3 All E.R. 38.

[2] L.G.A. 1972, s. 114.

[3] Employers' Liability (Compulsory Insurance) Act 1969.

Parish councils are empowered to insure against personal accidents, whether fatal or not, met with by their members while engaged on the business of the council.[1] Any sum received by the council under such insurance, after deduction of expenses of recovery, if any, is to be paid to the member concerned or his personal representatives. Insurances may also be taken out for voluntary assistants.[2]

Regular attention to insurance cover in the light of inflation is essential and, as a matter of good practice, insurance cover review should be on the agenda for the annual meeting of the council. Particular care should be taken where the insurance cover is piecemeal, since parish councils often find to their cost that some item which was thought to be covered, e.g. impact damage, is not, in fact, covered.

INTEREST IN CONTRACT OR OTHER MATTERS

(See Code of Conduct)

INVESTMENT

Any capital monies held by a parish council as the result of any sale of property, or the establishment of any fund (*see* "Funds and Accumulations") may, pending its use for statutory purposes, be invested in statutory securities, which means any security in which trustees are authorised by law to invest trust monies.[3] There is an obligation to pay into the capital fund such a sum as equals the income arising from it.

---

[1] L.G.A. 1972, s. 140(1) as substituted by L.G.(M.P.)A. 1982, s. 39(1).
[2] L.G.A. 1972, s. 140A, inserted by L.G.(M.P.)A. 1982, s. 39(2).
[3] L.G.A. 1972, Sch. 13, para. 16, and see Trustee Investments Act 1961.

JOINT COMMITTEES
(See also Interest in Contract or Other Matters)

A parish council may arrange with any other local authority with which it has, or may obtain, concurrent powers, for the appointment of a joint committee for the purpose of exercising a function,[1] and such a committee may have all the powers of an appointing council except the power to borrow, or to precept for a rate.[2]

Every member of a joint committee who at the time of his appointment was a member of the parish council or other appointing authority, upon ceasing to be a member of the appointing authority, ceases also to be a member of the joint committee.[3]

The expenses of the joint committee are defrayed by the councils by whom the joint committee is appointed in such proportions as they may agree upon, or as may be determined in case of difference by the district or unitary council, if the joint committee comprises only parish councils, or in any other case by a single arbitrator agreed upon by the appointing authorities, or in default of agreement, by the Secretary of State.[4]

The accounts of a joint committee are subject to audit as provided for by the Audit Commission Act 1998. (*See* "Audit".)

LAND

(See Allotments—Compulsory Purchase of Land— Information about Land—Property of Parish Council— Untidy Land)

---

[1] L.G.A. 1972, s. 102.
[2] L.G.A. 1972, s. 101(6).
[3] L.G.A. 1972, s. 102(5).
[4] L.G.A. 1972, s. 103.

LAUNDERETTES

(See Baths, etc.)

LAVATORIES, PUBLIC

(See Public Conveniences)

LEGAL ADVICE

Legal advice is provided free of charge by the National Association of Local Councils (109 Great Russell Street, London, WC1B 3LD) and the Local Councils Advisory Service (3 Trinity Close, 20 Church Street, Henley-on-Thames, Oxon., RG9 1SE) for subscribing member councils. Advice may also be sought from solicitors on a fee-paying basis.

As an incident of the functions with which Parliament has entrusted them, parish councils may incur reasonable expenses on any legal matters relating to any of their powers and duties. To this end the parish council may wish to engage a local solicitor. This is particularly important where the matter has progressed beyond the advice stage, and proceedings are envisaged (*see* "Legal Proceedings"), or takes the form of a land transaction, or requires detailed local examination or prolonged local involvement.

LEGAL PROCEEDINGS

(See *also* Public Inquiries)

Where a parish council considers it expedient for the promotion or protection of the interest of the inhabitants of the parish, it may prosecute or defend or appear in any legal proceedings.[1]

---

[1] L.G.A. 1972, s. 222(1)(a).

The clerk, or any other officer or member authorised generally, or in respect of any particular matter, by resolution of the parish council, may institute or defend or appear on its behalf in proceedings before any magistrates' court.[1] Any member or officer so authorised shall be entitled to institute or defend such proceedings and to conduct the proceedings although he is not a practising solicitor.[2]

A parish council may appear and represent its inhabitants at any public or local inquiry held by any government department or public body under any Act.[3] (*See* "Public Inquiries".)

For action in respect of damage to street furniture, *see* "Damage".

LEGAL PROCEEDINGS IN RESPECT OF DISQUALIFICATIONS

(See Disqualifications for Office of Parish Councillor)

LIBRARIES

(See Public Libraries, Museums and Art Galleries)

LICENCES

Where a district or unitary council proposes to adopt powers relating to the issue of hackney carriage licences, it must first inform the parish council.[4]

If the parish council is proposing to organise a public event,

---

[1] L.G.A. 1972, s. 111.
[2] L.G.A. 1972, s. 223.
[3] L.G.A. 1972, s. 222(1)(b).
[4] L.G.A. 1972, Sch. 14, para. 25; L.G.(M.P.)A. 1976, s. 45.

e.g. a dance, theatre, etc., or any public function involving the sale of intoxicating liquor, it must take care to obtain any necessary licence.

Applicants seeking a new liquor licence or the ordinary or special removal or transfer of a licence, or orders to extend existing drinking hours in a restaurant where dancing or other entertainment is allowed, are required to notify the parish council.

LIFE-SAVING APPARATUS

A parish council is empowered to provide life-saving appliances at such places, whether used for bathing or not, as it thinks fit.[1]

LIGHTING

For any highway which is the responsibility of the highway authority, the power of providing road lighting rests with the highway authority.[2] Road lighting is any lighting other than footway lighting (*see below*). On the 1st April 1967, all road lighting in a parish was transferred to the highway authority.[3] This included all lamps and other apparatus.

Usually the highway authority will be the county council and road lighting powers can be delegated by that authority to a lighting authority (i.e. a district council or parish council). The lighting authority acts as agent for the highway authority, which can control all aspects of work and expenditure.[4]

---

[1] P.H.A. 1936, s. 234, and L.G.A. 1972, Sch. 14, para. 18.
[2] H.A. 1980, s. 97.
[3] H.A. 1980, s. 270.
[4] H.A. 1980, s. 98.

Where there is a unitary council, the highway authority will be that council, and powers of delegation will be restricted to the parish council as lighting authority.

Footway lighting is lighting where either no lamp is more than 13 feet above the ground or no lamp is more than 20 feet above ground and there is at least one space exceeding 50 yards between two adjacent lights in the system. This definition can be altered by Ministerial Order.[1]

A parish council is a lighting authority and may provide footway lighting.[2] The parish council may, for the purpose of lighting the roads and other public places, provide and maintain such lamps, lamp posts and other materials and apparatus as it thinks necessary, and erect or install them on or against any premises or in other convenient places. The parish council may contract with any person for the supply of gas, electricity or other means of lighting, and may employ persons for maintenance and superintendence, with or without remuneration. (For the definition of "road", *see* "Roads".) Before installing any *new* system of footway lighting, the parish council must obtain the consent of the highway authority, and this consent may be given without conditions, or subject to such conditions as the highway authority thinks fit.[3]

Where the district council, or if there is no district council, the county council, exercises lighting powers in a parish or part thereof, its expenses are charged to the whole district, or county as the case may be, unless the district (or county) council by resolution declares the expenses to be "special expenses" chargeable separately on that parish or part (*see* "Expenses").

---

[1] H.A. 1980, s. 270.
[2] P.C.A. 1957, s. 3, and L.G.A. 1972, Sch. 14, para. 34.
[3] H.A. 1980, s. 301.

There are two cases in which a parish council exercising footway lighting powers can compel the highway authority to take over its existing lighting. First, it can alter its system so that it ceases to conform to the definition of footway lighting (*see above* for definition). The second is if the highway authority proposes to provide road lighting along the same stretch as is covered by existing footway lighting and gives notice accordingly.[1]

A parish council can also light an open space under its control.[2] The conditions applicable to footway lighting do not apply.

The carrying out of the lighting powers may be exercised by a committee or officer appointed by the parish council (*see* "Agency").

The installation of lighting apparatus is subject to various consents (*see* "Consents, etc. under the Parish Councils Act 1957"); and to the same provisions relating to access to telegraphic lines, sewers, etc. as apply to bus shelters (*see* "Bus Shelters").

The parish council may fix lights or wires to a building with the consent of the owner (which includes a tenant with at least five years of his tenancy left). The owner may require the temporary removal of the equipment during reconstruction or repair of the building, and a fresh owner can require their permanent removal. If the council think a requirement of permanent removal is unreasonable they may apply to a magistrates' court who may extend the period of notice allowed, or permit the permanent retention of the equipment either unconditionally or subject to conditions (including provision for payment of rent). Where the building is an ancient

---

[1] H.A. 1980, s. 270.
[2] O.S.A. 1906, s. 10, and P.C.A. 1957, s. 8(1).

monument or an historic building, an appeal against a notice lies to the Secretary of State and where it is owned by certain public bodies, the appeal lies to the appropriate Minister.[1]

Where damage is caused by negligence to any lighting apparatus, the parish council may take proceedings for damages, either in the magistrates' court or the county court, depending on the sum involved. On a prosecution for criminal damage, a magistrates' court may, on conviction, order the offender to pay compensation in addition to any fine or other punishment (*see* "Damage").

A parish council may combine with any other parish council for the purpose of exercising these powers, e.g. in relation to a road forming the boundary between the parishes; may contribute towards the expenses of any other council in the exercise of such powers; and may contribute towards the reasonable expenses incurred by any person in providing public lighting.

Where the lighting powers are exercised in part of a parish only, the rate levied for this purpose may, by resolution of the parish council, be charged on that part of the parish only.[2]

A parish council may borrow money for public lighting purposes (*see* "Loans to Parish Council").

Basically a stretch of road which is lighted by lamps not more than 200 yards apart is automatically subject to a speed limit, but the Road Traffic Acts contain provisions for modifying this rule in relation to particular stretches of road. In practice these modifications frequently apply.

---

[1] P.H.A. 1961. s. 45.
[2] L.G.A. 1972, Sch. 13, para. 25.

LIMITS UPON THE POWERS OF THE PARISH COUNCIL

This book notes all the various powers possessed by parish councils. A parish council is a body constituted under powers conferred by Parliament and it only has the powers which Parliament has specifically conferred upon it by Acts of Parliament.

From time to time, a parish council is pressed to undertake an activity for which Parliament has not directly conferred the necessary powers—for example, to undertake a postcard poll of the views of residents on some public issue. If the council is satisfied that what is proposed is for the benefit of the area or its inhabitants, it may be able to use its power to incur minor expenditure (*see* "Free Resource"), but the proposal may be on too large a scale for that. Sometimes the proposed activity is not within the powers of *any* local authority. In such a case, the only course is to advise those who press for this undertaking accordingly, and refer them to their Member of Parliament. In other cases, Parliament has conferred the powers upon some other local authority than the parish council, usually the district council or the county council, and the powers have not been delegated to the parish council. In such a case it is important to make plain to those who demand action with which local authority the responsibility lies. If the members of the parish council are sufficiently impressed with the need for the proposed provision, it is open to the chairman to communicate with the chairman of the appropriate committee of the local authority concerned.

The sympathy and interest of the appropriate member for the area on the district council or the county council can very properly be sought.

Owing to the powers of delegation which may or may not be

118

used in any particular area and the fact that there has been an increase in concurrent powers, i.e. powers which may be exercised by either authority, it is not easy to set out briefly the respective responsibilities of the principal councils, i.e. the county council and the district council. But, in general, the county council deals with education, highways and private streets, police, fire, personal social services, youth employment, libraries, consumer protection, refuse disposal and small holdings. The district council is responsible for housing, environmental health and nuisances, by-laws, clean air, planning applications, building regulations, coast protection, markets, refuse collection, the Council Tax and rating.

However, the arrival of unitary authorities in England as a consequence of the Local Government Act 1992 means that a single authority, being either a county council or a district council, will combine all the above functions.

In most instances the district council (or county council if there is no district council) has powers concurrently with the parish council. Unless there is a specific provision to the contrary, any of the functions of a county or district council may be delegated to a parish council (*see* "Agency").

LITIGATION

(See Damage—Legal Proceedings—Public Inquiries)

LITTER

(See *also* Untidy Land)

Legislation in respect of litter is now consolidated in the Environmental Protection Act 1990. It is a criminal offence for any person to drop or deposit any litter within the parish in, into, or from any place to which the public are entitled to or permitted to have access without payment, provided that it is in the open air or in a covered place open to the air on at least one side (such as a bus shelter).[1] If the parish council decides to prosecute, the council may resolve that any member or officer (whether or not he is a lawyer) may appear on its behalf in a magistrates' court (*see* "Legal Proceedings").

The maximum fine is fixed at level 4 on the standard scale (currently £2,500) and the court should take into account the nature of the litter and any danger which it presents to persons or animals. A parish council, with a view to promoting the abatement of litter, may take such steps as it considers appropriate to advise the public of these litter laws.

A parish council may provide litter bins in any street or public place. If it does so, it must empty and cleanse them so that the contents shall not become a nuisance or give reasonable ground for complaint. Anywhere where it may provide bins it may put up notices about the leaving of refuse and litter.

It may also cleanse and empty litter bins provided by anyone else. The county and district councils have similar powers, so where it is convenient for one authority to provide the bins and another to empty them this can be done. It should, however, be noted that the authority which provides the bins has a duty to empty them.

The county council may contribute to the expenses of the parish council in this regard. The parish council may contribute to the reasonable expenses incurred by anyone else in doing anything which the parish council could do under these provisions and two parish councils may combine for the purpose of exercising these powers, or one may contribute to the expenses of another.

The Secretary of State has advised local authorities that the

---

[1] Environmental Protection Act 1990, s. 87.

design of litter bins should be of a high standard. Some firms will provide bins free in return for a right to place an advertisement on them; such advertisements need to be considered for their effect on amenity, but in many places they will not be harmful to amenity if placed inside and just below the rim at the back, where they can be seen by persons depositing litter in the bin.

The dumping on any land in the open air (even on another's private land) or on a highway, of a motor vehicle or any part thereof, or on any such land anything other than a motor vehicle, is an offence for which the maximum penalty is a fine at level 3 on the standard scale for summary offences (currently £1,000) or 3 months' imprisonment or both. A parish council may prosecute.[1] The district or unitary council must provide places for the free dumping of rubbish.[2] The district or unitary council must deal with abandoned motor vehicles and may remove other dumped refuse.[3]

LOANS TO PARISH COUNCIL

In the past, a parish council wishing to embark on any capital project was usually compelled to borrow money because of the impossibility of establishing a capital fund. Funds are now possible (*see* "Funds and Accumulations") but the need to borrow will still occur in many cases.

In general, a parish council may borrow money for any purpose or class of purpose approved by the Secretary of State, and in accordance with any conditions subject to which the approval is given.[4]

---

[1] Refuse Disposal (Amenity) Act 1978, s. 2.

[2] *ibid*., s. 1.

[3] *ibid*., ss. 3 to 6 as amended by L.G.P.L.A. 1980, s. 1(3) and Sch. 3, paras, 14-16.

[4] L.G.A. 1972, Sch. 13–borrowing by local authorities–paras. 1-12.

In practice, applications for loans in England should be made to the National Association of Local Councils through the County Association, since the Secretary of State has delegated administration of loan applications to the Association.

There was formerly a ceiling on the total amount councils could borrow in any one financial year. That ceiling has been abolished but an individual council will not normally be authorised to borrow more than £500,000 in a single year.

In Wales, the system is slightly different. A council may apply either through its Association or direct to the Local Government Finance Division of the National Assembly for Wales. There is no specific limit to the amount a council may borrow but the National Assembly may set an annual cash limit on the total available for borrowing.

Money can be raised in various ways—by mortgage, the issue of stock, etc., by an agreement with the U.K. Debt Management Office and by any other means approved by the Secretary of State. Mostly, councils borrow from the Public Works Loans Board which operates (as does the Debt Management Office) from Eastcheap Court, 11 Philpot Lane, London, EC3M 8UD (website www.pwlb.gov.uk).

Reborrowing for the purpose of paying monies borrowed, or borrowing by way of temporary loan or overdraft from a bank or otherwise pending the receipt of revenue or authorised loan capital, does not require the approval of the Secretary of State.

All money borrowed by a parish council must be charged indifferently on all the revenues of the authority, and all securities created rank equally without any priority.

Two or more local authorities may combine to exercise their powers of borrowing.

The Secretary of State may make regulations on matters of detail relating to borrowing.

LOCAL ACT POWERS

The powers and duties of parish councils set out in this book are those contained in the general law. It should not be forgotten, however, that some parish councils have, in addition, power conferred on them by Private Acts. Parish councils have no power themselves to promote Bills in Parliament (*see* "Bills in Parliament"), but local Bills promoted by other local authorities may contain provisions conferring powers on parish councils. In recent years a number of parish councils have obtained powers not available under the general law, under county council Acts. The 1972 Act provided for then existing Local Acts to be phased out but Local Acts passed after 1st April 1974 remain in force. (*See* "Bills in Parliament".)

LOCAL AUTHORITIES MUTUAL INVESTMENT TRUST

(See Investment)

LOCAL GOVERNMENT ELECTORS

The local government electors for an area are those whose names are registered in the current register of local government electors.[1] These registers are generally combined with the registers of parliamentary electors, the names of those registered only as local government electors being specially marked.

The register is published annually no later than 1st December but subsequent changes are made as they occur, thus creating

---

[1] L.G.A. 1972, s. 270.

a "rolling" register that is always up to date. A person is entitled to be included in the next register if he is resident in any local government area and he is a British subject,[1] citizen of the Republic of Ireland or a citizen of a member state of the European Union of full age (eighteen) or who will attain full age before the end of twelve months beginning with the 1st December next and is not subject to any legal incapacity to vote. His right to vote, however, depends on his achieving full age by the election day. If a local government area is divided into wards, he can only vote for the ward in which he resides. If the place at which he resides is covered by two or three different local government authorities, e.g. a county council, a district council and a parish council, he is, of course, entitled to vote at elections for all these bodies.

Those who are registered as service voters can vote by proxy. Absent voters may vote by post or by proxy.[2]

Only local government electors are entitled to speak and vote at a parish meeting. Non-electors may be invited or permitted to speak, but not to vote.

LOCAL OMBUDSMAN

(See Commission for Local Administration)

LOTTERIES

A parish council may run a lottery,[3] provided it is conducted in accordance with a scheme registered with the Gaming Board. The Board provides guidance pamphlets and forms. Its address is Berkshire House, 168-173 High Holborn, London, WC1V 7AA.

---

[1] Which includes Commonwealth citizens.
[2] R.P.A. 1985, s. 8.
[3] Lotteries and Amusements Act 1976.

MAYOR

(See Chairman of Parish Council)

MEETINGS OF PARISH COUNCIL

(See *also* Annual Meeting of Parish Council—Chairman of Parish Council —Interest in Contract or Other Matters—Parish Council—Quorum)

Frequency

A parish council in England must hold not less than four meetings in each year, of which one is to be the annual meeting.[1] A community council in Wales must hold the annual meeting and may hold such additional meetings as it thinks fit.[2]

Open to the public

Every meeting is to be open to the public except where the council formally resolve to exclude the public (which includes the Press) from all or part of a meeting on the grounds that publicity would be prejudicial to the public interest by reason of the confidential nature of the business to be transacted or for other special reasons stated in the resolution and arising from the nature of the business or of the proceedings.[3] This provision applies equally to any committee of the parish council[4] and to the parish meeting. The resolution (which could be challenged in the courts) must be carefully worded and reported verbatim in the minutes.

The public cannot be excluded simply on the chairman's ruling. The decision must be taken by the council. It is unwise

---

[1] L.G.A. 1972, Sch. 12, para. 8.

[2] *ibid.*, para. 24.

[3] Public Bodies (Admission to Meetings) Act 1960, s. 1.

[4] L.G.A. 1972, s. 100.

to exclude the public or Press unless it is considered absolutely necessary since this can give rise to bad feeling and allegations of secrecy. Exclusion should be strictly limited to the period during which the specific issue which requires confidential discussion is being considered.

Where a meeting is to be open to the public, the Press must, if they ask, be given in advance a copy of the agenda and any supporting documents. From a public relations point of view it is good practice to do this even if they do not ask.

Members of the public have no rights to speak at a parish council meeting unless the council (not the chairman) authorises this. A district councillor has no special rights above those of an ordinary member of the public.

The Local Government (Access to Information) Act 1985 (contained in Part VA of the Local Government Act 1972) does not apply to parish councils as a matter of law, but they may adopt all or part of its provisions if they so wish.

Convening

The chairman may call a meeting of the parish council at any time. Any two members may present a requisition to the chairman to convene a meeting. If the chairman thereafter refuses to call a meeting, any two members may forthwith convene one. If, without refusing, the chairman does not within seven days after the requisition convene a meeting, any two members may forthwith convene a meeting.[1]

Notices

Three clear days[2] at least before a meeting of the parish council, a notice specifying the time and place of meeting must be

---

[1] L.G.A. 1972, Sch. 12, paras. 9 and 25.
[2] Saturdays and Sundays are *not* excluded.

posted at the offices of the council, or if it has no offices, in some conspicuous place in the parish,[1] and a summons sent to each member. If the meeting is called by members of the council, the notice must specify the business to be transacted, and must be signed by those members. A summons to attend the meeting, specifying the business to be transacted, signed by the clerk, must be left at or sent by post to the usual place of residence of every member of the council three clear days at least before the meeting. The period of three clear days is exclusive of the day on which the notice is given and the day on which the meeting is held.[2] (*See* "Notices, etc.".) Want of service of the summons on any member does not affect the validity of a meeting.

In view of the above provisions (which are statutory), it is undesirable to discuss any business of substantial importance of which notice has not been given. In particular, no *decision* can lawfully be taken on any matter not specified in the summons, e.g. which arises under "any other business". It is useful for standing orders to specify this point to avoid difficulties.

Place

A meeting of the parish council must not be held on premises licensed for the sale of intoxicating liquor, except when no other suitable room is available free of charge or at a reasonable charge. There is nothing to prevent the meetings being held outside the boundaries of the parish if the council consider this course desirable.[3]

When there is no suitable public room which can be used free of charge, the parish council is entitled to use, free of

---

[1] Public Bodies (Admissions to Meetings) Act 1960, s. 1(4).

[2] L.G.A. 1972, Sch. 12, paras. 10 and 26.

[3] *ibid.*

charge, at all reasonable times and after reasonable notice for the purpose of a meeting of the parish council, any suitable room in a community, foundation or voluntary school, or any suitable room the expense of maintaining which is payable out of any rate. (*See* "Rooms in School and Rooms Maintained out of Rates".)

A parish council is empowered to provide or acquire buildings for public offices and for public meetings. (*See* "Public or Parish Offices".)

There is no legal reason why a meeting should not take place in a private house but the practice is undesirable since the council is conducting public business.

Quorum

No business is to be transacted at any meeting of a parish council unless at least one-third of the full number of members are present. In no case, however, can the quorum be less than three. (*See further* "Quorum".)

Minutes

Minutes of the proceedings of every parish council or of any committee thereof are to be kept in a book.[1] The minutes should be kept by the clerk. If there is no clerk, some person should be authorised by the council or committee for the purpose. Minutes should be short. In general terms they should record decisions, not the discussions which precede them. The council minutes must be signed at the same or the next ensuing meeting of the council by the presiding chairman. A loose leaf book may be used provided that the pages are consecutively numbered and each page is initialled by the chairman when the minutes are signed. This facilitates the typing of minutes. Questions sometimes arise as to the printing

---

[1] L.G.A. 1972, Sch. 12, para. 41.

of the council's minutes and reports. The circulated papers in the larger local authorities are voluminous and printing is largely used for this purpose. There is nothing to prevent a parish council taking the same course where the circumstances warrant it. For inspection of minutes, *see* "Inspection of Documents".

Procedure

The names of members present at any council meeting must be recorded.[1] Any member may move a resolution of a matter on the agenda, which should then be discussed and voted upon. The extent and length of discussion is a matter for the chairman who should exercise a careful but firm balance between ensuring full and relevant discussions, and avoiding verbosity, irrelevant matter and repetitiveness. A seconder to a resolution is not essential, unless standing orders so provide. Except in very straightforward cases, the resolution should be noted in writing by the clerk before voting takes place to avoid the possibility of subsequent misunderstandings as to the wording. The mode of voting *must* be by show of hands unless otherwise provided in standing orders.[2] The names of members voting on each question must also be recorded on the requisition of any member of the council, so as to show whether each vote given was for or against the question. Hence a vote cannot be taken by secret ballot, unless standing orders so provide.

Every question must be decided by a majority of the members present and voting on the question.[3] In the case of an equal division of votes, the chairman has a second or casting vote. The chairman has an original as well as a casting vote. The manner in which each member voted must be recorded in

---

[1] L.G.A. 1972, Sch. 12, para. 40.

[2] *ibid.*, paras. 13 and 29.

[3] *ibid.*, para. 39.

the minutes if any member so requires either before or after the vote is taken.

A parish council may make, vary and revoke standing orders or the regulation of its proceedings and business, and of the proceedings and business at parish meetings. (*See* "Standing Orders".)

As regards disorderly conduct at meetings of parish councils, every deliberative body is empowered at common law to protect itself in its deliberations, and if these deliberations are materially obstructed by the disorderly conduct of any person thereat, whether a stranger or a member, the general body, acting through the chairman, is justified in removing that obstruction by requiring such person to leave the meeting, and if such requisition be not obeyed, by using such an amount of force as may be necessary to compel his retirement. It is desirable that any force which it may be necessary to use in any case of this kind should be applied, where the opportunity offers, by a police constable. The parish council must determine for itself how far in any particular instance there may or may not be such conduct as materially obstructs the deliberations of the council.

MEETINGS, PARISH OR COMMUNITY

(See Parish Meetings)

MEMBERS' INTERESTS

(See Code of Conduct)

MEMORIALS

(See War Memorials)

MINOR AND MISCELLANEOUS EXPENSES

(See Free Resource)

MINUTES

(See Meetings of Parish Council)

MONUMENTS

(See Burial and Cremation)

MORTGAGES

(See Loans to Parish Council)

MORTUARIES AND POST-MORTEM ROOMS

A parish council may, and if required by the Secretary of State must, provide—(a) a mortuary for the reception of dead bodies before interment; (b) a post-mortem room for the reception of dead bodies during the time required to conduct any post-mortem examination ordered by a coroner; and it may make by-laws with respect to the management, and charge for the use of any such place.[1] (*See* "By-laws".)

The council may provide for the interment of any dead body received into its mortuary, but the burial expenses are chargeable to the deceased's estate.

As to obtaining a loan, *see* "Loans to Parish Council".

Except in large parishes, mortuaries are usually provided by the district or unitary council which has the like powers and

---

[1] P.H.A. 1936, s. 198.

duties. Where it appears to the district or unitary council that no suitable arrangements have been made for the disposal of the body of a person who has died or been found dead in its area, it is the duty of that district council to arrange for the body to be buried or cremated.[1]

MOTOR-CYCLE PARKS

(See Parking Places)

MUSEUMS AND ART GALLERIES

A parish council may contribute to a local museum or art gallery through its powers to contribute to the arts (*see* "Entertainment and the Arts").

NAME OF PARISH

(See *also* Signs and Signposts)

The district or unitary council may change the name of a parish at the request of the parish council, or of the parish meeting where there is no parish council. The change of name must be published in such manner as the district or unitary council directs and must be notified to the Secretary of State, the Director General of the Ordnance Survey and the Registrar General.[2]

A change of name will not affect any rights or obligations of the parish, or any pending legal proceedings.

NAMING OF STREETS

(See Numbering of Houses)

---

[1] Public Health (Control of Disease) Act 1984, s. 46.
[2] L.G.A. 1972, s. 75.

NATIONAL ASSOCIATION OF LOCAL COUNCILS

The main representative body for parish councils is the National Association of Local Councils, 109 Great Russell Street, London, WC1B 3LD, founded in 1947. It has county associations in every county (or group of counties) in England and Wales.

NATIONAL INSURANCE

(See Employees)

NATIONAL PARK AUTHORITIES

In England, the Secretary of State is required to appoint a certain number of National Park Authority members from among parish councillors, and chairmen of parish meetings without councils, whose parishes are wholly or partly within National Park boundaries. The maximum number is one less than half the total number of Authority members appointed by the Secretary of State. As a general rule, just under half the Authority members are appointed by the Secretary of State, with the majority being appointed by the principal local authorities within the area of the National Park.[1]

The Secretary of State is not required to appoint community councillors as members of National Park Authorities in Wales.

NOISE

(See also Nuisances and Pollution)

District and unitary councils have wide general powers to act against noise or vibration which is a nuisance. These powers

---

[1] Environment Act 1995, s. 63 and Sch. 7.

can by agreement be exercised by a parish council (*see* "Agency"). It is an offence to use loudspeakers in streets at night (i.e. between 9 p.m. and 8 a.m.) for any purpose, or at any time for commercial advertising or advertising entertainments subject to exceptions in the case of mobile shops selling perishable foods between noon and 7 p.m., so long as they do not give reasonable cause for annoyance to persons in the vicinity. There are a number of exclusions from these prohibitions, ranging from police loudspeakers, loudspeakers hailing a ship and pleasure fair loudspeakers, to ordinary car radios. For offences concerning loudspeakers, the parish council has power to prosecute.[1]

The district or unitary council has powers to control the use of loudspeakers in streets by adopting Schedule 2 to the Noise and Statutory Nuisance Act 1993, under which it operates a licensing system.

Under the Noise Act 1996, a district or unitary council may adopt the provisions of the Act and thus give themselves powers to deal with complaints about excessive noise from dwellings at night (between 11 p.m. and 7 a.m.).

Advice may be sought from the Noise Abatement Society, 44 Grand Parade, Brighton, East Sussex, BN2 9QA.

NOTICES BY OR TO PARISH COUNCIL OR OF PARISH MEETING

(See *also* Meetings of Parish Council—Parish Meeting)

Any public notice required to be given by a parish council must be given by posting the notice in some conspicuous place or places in the parish and in such other manner as

---

[1] Control of Pollution Act 1974, s. 62.

appears to the parish council to be desirable for giving publicity to the notice, e.g. leaflets, advertisements in local paper, etc.[1]

A public notice of a parish meeting (which may be in writing or in print, or partly in writing and partly in print) must be given as above and must specify the time and place of the meeting and the business to be transacted at the meeting, and it must be posted up seven clear days before the meeting— that is, exclusive of the day of giving the notice and the day on which the meeting is to be held. If, in England, the business relates to the establishment or dissolution of a parish council, or the grouping of a local area with another local area, not less than fourteen days' notice must be given. In Wales, there are special rules relating to the calling of meetings to consider the establishment and dissolution of community councils and the grouping of communities (*see* "Parish Council – Creation of community council in Wales *and* Dissolution of community council in Wales"). The duty of giving public notice of the meeting is imposed on the chairman of the parish council, or on the conveners of the meeting, as the case may be.[2]

Public notice is required to be given by a parish council as to the audit of their accounts. (*See* "Audit".)

Three clear days at least before a meeting of the parish council, a notice must be given as above and a summons, specifying the business proposed to be transacted and signed by the clerk, left at or sent by post to the residence of every parish councillor.[3] (*See also* "Meetings of Parish Council".)

Any notice required to be given to or served on a parish council, or to or upon the clerk or chairman, shall be addressed to the council and left at or sent by prepaid post to the offices

---

[1] L.G.A. 1972, s. 232.

[2] L.G.A. 1972, Sch. 12, paras. 15 and 30.

[3] *ibid.*, paras. 10 and 26.

of the council.[1] In the case of notices required to be given to or served on a parish meeting, or the chairman of a parish meeting, these should be addressed to the chairman of the parish meeting at his private address.

Notice is required to be given to a parish council by a district or unitary council of the particulars of any planning application in the area of the parish council, provided the local council has requested to be notified of all such applications. (*See* "Planning".)

Parish councils and the chairmen of parish meetings in England without councils are entitled to be notified of public path creation, diversion and extinguishment orders and of orders modifying the definitive map (*see* "Highways").

Notice is required to be given by the district or unitary council to a parish council and to the chairman of a parish meeting in England without a council of the exercise of regulatory powers relating to Hackney Carriage licences (*see* "Licences"), by-laws for promenades and the seashore and street naming.[2]

Notice is to be given to the chairman of the council of any resignation by a parish councillor (*see* "Parish Councillor"), and a notice is to be given to the council by the chairman in the event of his resigning his chairmanship (*see* "Chairman of Parish Council").[3]

NUISANCES AND POLLUTION

(*See also* Ditches and Drains—Noise)

Nuisances and cases of pollution should be reported to the district or unitary council for attention and action. If, however,

---

[1] L.G.A. 1972, s. 231.
[2] L.G.A. 1972, Sch. 14, para. 25.
[3] L.G.A. 1972, s. 84.

the district or unitary council refuses to take appropriate action, the parish council has two reserve powers available to it under the Environmental Protection Act 1990, Part III. First, it may advise private persons particularly affected to take proceedings in a magistrates' court for an abatement order and, if the nuisance affects the parish in general, contribute to the costs of the private persons' court case out of the free resource. Second, it can report the failure to the Environment Agency, which has powers to investigate.

NUMBERING OF HOUSES AND NAMING OF STREETS

A parish council has no direct powers in this field, since it is a duty imposed on the district or unitary council.[1] The district or unitary council can arrange for the parish council to carry out this function, but only if the parish council agrees.[2] If this happens, the parish council acts as agent and the district or unitary council must pay the cost. The district or unitary council could, however, declare the expenses to be special expenses chargeable on the parish.

OBSTRUCTION OF HIGHWAY

(See Highways)

OFFICERS OF PARISH COUNCIL

(See Clerk of Parish Council—Deputy Officers—Employees—Gratuities to Officers—Legal Proceedings—Superannuation of Paid Officers—Treasurer of Parish Council)

---

[1] Town Improvement Clauses Act 1847, s. 64; P.H.A. 1925, ss. 17-19.
[2] L.G.A. 1972, s. 101.

OFFICES FOR PARISH COUNCIL

(See Land—Property of Parish Council—Public or Parish Offices)

OMBUDSMAN

(See Commission for Local Administration)

OPEN SPACES

The powers which may be exercised by a parish with respect to an "open space" which is under its control, or to the expense of which it has contributed, to however small an extent, are similar to those in respect of a recreation ground.[1] (*See* "Recreation".)

Under the Open Spaces Act 1906, trustees under a local Act may transfer any open space to a parish council so that the open space may be preserved for the enjoyment of the public, or may enter into an agreement with the parish council for the opening to the public of the open space and for the care and management of the same by the parish council.[2] Where an open space is vested in trustees for any charitable purpose, and the open space is no longer required for the purpose of the trust, the trustees may transfer the open space to the parish council.[3]

A parish council may acquire and undertake the management of any open space or disused burial ground.[4] It must maintain it in a good and decent state. Any land held by a parish council

---

[1] P.H.A. 1875, s. 164, and L.G.A. 1972, Sch. 14, para. 27.

[2] O.S.A. 1906, s. 2.

[3] O.S.A. 1906, s. 4.

[4] O.S.A. 1906, s. 9.

under the 1906 Act is held on a statutory trust for the public. This is not necessarily a charitable trust.[1]

A parish council may make by-laws for the regulation of any open space. (*See* "By-laws".)

An "open space" is defined in the Act of 1906 as "any land, whether enclosed or not, on which there are no buildings or of which not more than one-twentieth part is covered with buildings, and the whole or the remainder of which is laid out as a garden or is used for purposes of recreation, or lies waste and unoccupied".[2] Several of the provisions of the Act also apply to disused burial grounds.

A parish council may borrow money for the purposes of the Act of 1906. (*See* "Loans to Parish Council".)

The address of the Open Spaces Society, which body may be able to advise a council with a problem, is 25A Bell Street, Henley-on-Thames RG9 2BA.

PARISH

Subject to adjustments in a few cases, all rural parishes in England in existence immediately before the 1st April 1974 continue to exist as parishes,[3] together with those former urban districts or boroughs, or parts thereof, constituted as parishes by order of the Secretary of State with effect from the 1st April 1974.[4]

In Wales, all rural parishes in existence immediately before the 1st April 1974 ceased to exist as local areas, but were

---

[1] O.S.A. 1906, s. 10.
[2] O.S.A. 1906, s. 20.
[3] L.G.A. 1972, s. 1(6).
[4] L.G.A. 1972, Sch. 1, Part V.

reborn on that date under the name of communities (*see* "Community").

Since 1974 further changes have been made in respect of both parishes and communities as a result of reviews undertaken by the Local Government Commission and its successor, the Electoral Commission (see "Alteration of Areas").

PARISH COUNCIL

(See *also* Annual Meeting of Parish Council— Expenses—Grouping of Parishes—Legal Proceedings — Meetings of Parish Council—Parish Councillor— Quorum—Town Council)

Definition

There are over 9,000 parish and community councils in England and Wales.

These include, in England, parish councils whether separate or common which were already in existence on 1st April 1974,[1] former rural borough councils which became parish councils on that date, and former borough and urban district councils given "successor" status as parish councils by the Secretary of State.[2]

In Wales, these include former parish councils which became community councils on the 1st April 1974 and former borough and urban district councils which became community councils by order of the Secretary of State.[3] The term "parish council", as used herein, includes community councils unless otherwise stated.

---

[1] L.G.A. 1972, s. 9.
[2] L.G.A. 1972, Sch. 1, Part V.
[3] L.G.A. 1972, s. 27.

A parish council is a corporate body, but it is not necessary for it to have a common seal. Any parish council act which requires a seal, e.g. a deed of conveyance, should be signed and sealed by two members of the council.[1] A parish council is a local authority.[2] For a parish council becoming a town council, *see* "Town Council".

Creation of parish council in England

In any parish in England where no parish council exists, the district or unitary council must establish a parish council if the population includes 200 or more local government electors. If the population includes more than 150 but less than 200 electors, the district or unitary council must establish a parish council if the parish meeting resolves that one should be established. This power is discretionary if the parish is already grouped under a common parish council. Where the population includes not more than 150 local government electors, the district or unitary council may create a parish council if the parish meeting so resolves.[3]

For the creation of parishes and parish councils by petition, *see* "Alteration of Areas".

Creation of community council in Wales

A community meeting which does not have a separate council may apply to the county or county borough council for the establishment of a community council for the community. However, an application may only be made if (a) a poll of local government electors for the community has been held and (b) a majority of those voting in the poll supports the application. The decision to hold a poll must be made at a community meeting at which at least 30% of the electorate

---

[1] L.G.A. 1972, ss. 14 and 33.

[2] L.G.A. 1972, s. 270.

[3] L.G.A. 1972, s. 9.

or, if that number exceeds 300, at least 300 electors, are present. At least 30 clear days' notice of the meeting must be given.[1]

If the above conditions are met, the county or county borough council is obliged to establish the council by order and make provision for the election of councillors, etc.

Dissolution of parish council in England

Where in England the population of a parish having a separate parish council includes not more than 150 local government electors, the parish meeting may apply to the district council for that council to make an order dissolving the parish council. If such an application is rejected, a further application cannot be made for two years.[2]

Dissolution of community council in Wales

The procedure for dissolving a community council is essentially the same as for its creation and, if successfully followed, obliges the county or county borough council to dissolve the community council and make provision for the winding up of its affairs.

If a proposal to create or dissolve a community council is rejected in a poll, a further poll cannot be held for at least two years. Furthermore, such a proposal cannot be made for two years (a) after changes made to the communities in question following a review by the Local Government Boundary Commission for Wales, or (b) following a successful application for a creation or a dissolution order.[3]

Size of council

A parish council in England consists of such number of

---

[1] L.G.A. 1972, ss. 28-29B, Sch. 12, para. 30(2).
[2] L.G.A. 1972, s. 10.
[3] L.G.A. 1972, ss. 28-30.

councillors as may be fixed from time to time by the district or unitary council, not being less than five.[1] Oddly enough, there is no similar provision for fixing the size of a community council in Wales but in practice it is not less than five.

If a casual vacancy arises, the parish council must fill the vacancy by co-option, except that there must be a by-election if a poll is claimed (*see* "Election of Parish Councillors").

The proceedings of a council are not to be invalidated by any vacancy among the members, or by any defect in the election or qualification of any of the members.[2]

For changes to the size of a council through a review by a Local Government Commission, *see* "Alteration of Areas".

PARISH COUNCILLOR

**(See *also* Allowances to Parish Councillors—
Disqualifications for Office of Parish Councillor—
Election of Parish Councillors—Interest in Contract or
Other Matters—Meetings of Parish Council)**

A parish councillor must be aged 21 years or over, be a British subject,[3] a citizen of the Irish Republic or a citizen of a member state of the European Union and be (1) a local government elector of the parish; or (2) a person who (a) has, during the whole of the twelve months before he was nominated as a candidate, occupied land or other premises as owner or tenant in the parish, or (b) has, during the same period, resided in that area or within three miles thereof, or (c) has, during the same period, had his principal or only place of work in that area.[4]

---

[1] L.G.A. 1972, s. 16(1).
[2] L.G.A. 1972, s. 82.
[3] Which includes a Commonwealth citizen.
[4] L.G.A. 1972, s. 79.

It has been decided that, in order to constitute residence, a person must possess at least a sleeping apartment, but that an uninterrupted abiding at such dwelling is not essential. A person may be resident in more than one place at the same time, e.g. a college student.[1] "Work" includes the performance of the duties of a councillor, so that a councillor seeking re-election qualifies as a candidate by virtue of acting as a councillor.[2]

Where a member of the council ceases to be qualified to be a member, the council must forthwith declare his office vacant and signify the vacancy by notice signed by the clerk and publicly notified (*see* "Notices").

As to who are local government electors, *see* "Local Government Electors".

In the case of parish councils in England, the number of councillors must not be less than five as may be fixed from time to time by the district council.

For the election and term of office of a parish councillor and the position if casual vacancies arise, *see* "Election of Parish Councillors".

A councillor, by notice in writing to the chairman (N.B. not to the clerk), may resign his office. Resignation takes effect on receipt of the notice by the chairman.[3]

Every parish councillor, before or at the next meeting after his election or, if the council at the first meeting so permits, then at a later meeting fixed by the council, must make in the presence of some member of the council or a proper officer of the council (i.e. usually the clerk) and deliver to the council a declaration of acceptance of office in the form prescribed

---

[1] *Fox v. Stirk* [1970] 2 Q.B. 463.

[2] *Parker v. Yeo* [1992] 90 L.G.R. 645.

[3] L.G.A. 1972, s. 84.

which includes an undertaking to observe the council's code of conduct in the performance of his duties (*see* " Code of Conduct").[1] If he fails to do so his office is void and a casual vacancy automatically arises.[2]

A parish councillor may be appointed as clerk or treasurer of the council *without remuneration*. A person who is or has been a member of the parish council is disqualified from being appointed by the council to any paid office whilst he is a member and for a period of twelve months after he has ceased to be a member.[3]

Parish councillors are not exempt from jury service.

As to the payments which may be made to parish councillors in respect of their personal expenses and financial losses as a result of council work, see "Allowances to Parish Councillors".

A person, if duly qualified, may be elected as a parish councillor for more than one parish or community.

A parish councillor has no personal financial liability in respect of anything done *in good faith* for the purpose of any of the council's statutory functions.[4]

PARISH MEETING

(*See also* Chairman of Parish Meeting— Community— Quorum—Wards)

Unless otherwise stated, what is set out below in respect of parish meetings applies to community meetings in Wales and town meetings in both England and Wales.

---

[1] L.G.A. 1972, s. 83 and L.G.A. 2000, s. 52.
[2] L.G.A. 1972, s. 83.
[3] L.G.A. 1972, s. 102.
[4] L.G.(M.P.)A. 1976, s. 39.

The persons entitled to speak and vote at a parish meeting are the persons registered as local government electors for the parish.[1]

The chairman of a parish council is entitled to attend a parish meeting for the parish (or where a grouping order is in force, for any of the parishes comprised in the group) whether or not he is a local government elector for the parish.[2] If the parish has a separate parish council, the chairman of that council, if present, shall preside at a parish meeting and, in the case of English meetings only, if he is absent the vice-chairman (if any) shall preside; but, if he is not a local government elector for the parish or community, he is not entitled to give any vote except a casting vote as chairman. In the absence of the chairman (in Wales) or the chairman and vice-chairman (in England) of the parish council, a parish meeting may appoint another person to take the chair for the occasion and that person has all the powers and authority of a chairman. (*See* "Chairman of Parish Meeting".)

In a parish in England not having a separate parish council, the parish meeting chooses a chairman for the year at its annual assembly (*see below*). If that chairman is absent from any meeting during that year, the meeting may appoint another person to take the chair and that person has all the powers and authority of a chairman. In a community in Wales not having a separate community council, the meeting must appoint a person for the occasion only. (*See* "Chairman of Parish Meeting".)

Members of the public (including the Press) may be present at the parish meeting, notwithstanding that they are not local government electors for the parish but have no right to take

---

[1] L.G.A. 1972, ss. 13(1) and 32(1).
[2] L.G.A. 1972, Sch. 12, paras. 16 and 31.

part in the business of the meeting.[1] They may only be excluded by a formal resolution of the parish meeting (for the circumstances in which the public can be excluded, *see* "Meetings of Parish Council").

The parish meeting in England must assemble annually on some day between 1st March and 1st June, both dates inclusive. In the case of a parish not having a separate parish council, the parish meeting must assemble at least twice a year. Subject to these rules, parish meetings in England may be held on such days and at such times and places as may be fixed by the parish council or, if there is no parish council, by the chairman of the parish meeting.[2] The community meeting in Wales is *not* required to assemble annually or at all. Proceedings at a parish meeting must not begin earlier than six o'clock in the evening.[3]

A parish meeting in England, but not a community meeting in Wales, may arrange for the discharge of any of its functions by a committee of local government electors for the parish but any such arrangement does not prevent the parish meeting itself from exercising these functions. The acts of a committee do not need ratification by the parish meeting.[4]

In England, the chairman of the parish council, or any two parish councillors or, if there is no parish council, the chairman of the parish meeting or any person representing the parish on the district council may convene a parish meeting, or any six local government electors may at any time convene a parish meeting.[5]

---

[1] Public Bodies (Admission to Meetings) Act 1960, s. 1.
[2] L.G.A. 1972, Sch. 12, para. 15.
[3] *ibid.*, paras. 14 and 32.
[4] L.G.A. 1972, s. 108
[5] L.G.A. 1972, Sch. 12, para. 15.

In Wales, the chairman of the community council or any two councillors of that council, or any six local government electors may at any time convene a community meeting.[1]

Seven clear days' (i.e. nine days') notice of the holding of a parish meeting must be given. If, in England, the business transacted relates to the establishment or dissolution of a parish council, or to the grouping of the parish with another parish under a common parish council, at least fourteen days' notice of the meeting must be given. In Wales, the law is different (*see* "Grouping of Parishes – Wales" and "Parish Councils – Creation and dissolution of community councils in Wales". The duty of giving public notice of the meeting is imposed on the chairman of the parish council, or on the conveners of the meeting, as the case may be. (*See* "Notices, etc.")

A parish meeting must not be held in premises licensed for the sale of intoxicating liquor, except where no other suitable room is available either free of charge or at a reasonable cost.[2] As to the use of schoolrooms, etc., *see* "Rooms in School and Rooms Maintained out of Rates".

Minutes of the proceedings of every parish meeting must be kept in a book provided for that purpose, and shall be signed at the same or the next ensuing assembly of the parish meeting or meeting of the committee, as the case may be, by the person presiding thereat. Until the contrary is proved, a parish meeting in respect of the proceedings of which a minute has been so made and signed is deemed to have been duly convened and held and all the persons present at the meeting are deemed to have been duly qualified.[3] Differences of opinion sometimes arise as to whether it is part of the duty of the clerk to the

---

[1] L.G.A. 1972, Sch. 12, para. 30.
[2] *ibid.*, paras. 14 and 32.
[3] *ibid.*, paras. 19 and 35.

parish council to take the minutes of a parish meeting. There is no simple answer to this, although a good working rule is that he is obliged to do so if it has been the practice for his predecessors to do so. The simplest solution is for the clerk to have a short written contract, specifying his duties as including the taking of minutes at parish or community meetings and, of course, for his pay to allow for this duty. If the clerk does not take the minutes, they should be taken by the chairman of the parish meeting or, under his direction, by some elector present at the meeting.

Every question is decided by the majority of those present and voting on the question. Each local government elector has the right to give one vote and no more on any question.[1] The decision announced by the chairman is final, unless a poll is demanded. (*See* "Polls".)

As to the expenses of a parish meeting or of the taking of a poll, *see* "Expenses and Expenditure" and "Polls".

For the powers of parish meetings in respect of the creation and dissolution of parish councils, *see* "Parish Council".

The parish meeting has a general power to discuss parish affairs[2] and pass resolutions thereon. Such resolutions will not bind the parish council. However, if a resolution that the council should provide allotments causes the council to be of the opinion that there is a demand for allotments, then the council has a duty to provide them.[3]

Where parishes are grouped under a common parish council, there must, nevertheless, be a separate parish meeting for every parish so grouped (*see* "Grouping of Parishes").

---

[1] L.G.A. 1972, Sch. 12, paras. 18 and 34.
[2] L.G.A. 1972, ss. 9 and 27.
[3] S.H.A.A. 1908, s. 23.

A parish meeting is not a corporate body nor for most purposes is it a local authority.[1] If there is no parish council its property vests, in the case of English parish meetings, in the parish trustees (*see* "Parish Trustees") and, in the case of Welsh community meetings, in the county or county borough council (*see* "Community").

A parish meeting in England where there is no council has some of the powers of a parish council (e.g. to provide allotments, to provide burial facilities, to appoint charity trustees, to maintain closed churchyards). In addition, the district or unitary council has power to confer on a parish meeting any function of a parish council.[2]

Not being a local authority for this purpose, a parish meeting cannot recover VAT on its purchases (*see* "Value Added Tax").

PARISH OFFICES

(See Public or Parish Offices)

PARISH PROPERTY

(See Property of Parish Council)

PARISH TRUSTEES

As from the 1st April 1974, the parish trustees replaced the former representative body in the case of English parishes where there is no parish council. The parish trustees consist of the chairman of the parish meeting and an official appointed by the district or unitary council. Together they constitute a

---

[1]   L.G.A. 1972, s. 270.
[2]   L.G.A. 1972, s. 109.

corporate body to hold the parish property.[1] They have no power to make any decisions of their own, but must act in accordance with any directions given to them by the parish meeting.[2]

The representative body in Wales was not replaced by community trustees and, accordingly, former parish property is vested in the county or county borough council on trust for the community (*see* "Community").

PARKING PLACES

(*See also* Commons—Village Greens)

Parish councils now have a general power to provide parking places for motor cars with the consent of the county or unitary council,[3] and may also, without consent, provide and maintain parking places for bicycles and motor-cycles (including structures for use as parking places, e.g. stands for bicycles) where it appears to them to be necessary to do so for the purpose of relieving or preventing congestion of traffic or preserving local amenities.[4]

For the purpose of providing cycle parks only (or for the provision of means of entrance and egress), the parish council may adopt and by order authorise the use of any part of a road within the parish or community. For the provision of any vehicle parks, it may utilise and adopt any land purchased for the purpose or appropriated as described below.

For the definition of "road", *see* "Roads".

The parish council may appropriate for the purpose of

---

[1] L.G.A. 1972, s. 13(3).
[2] L.G.A. 1972, s. 13(4).
[3] L.G.A. 1972, Sch. 19, para. 22.
[4] R.T.R.A. 1984, s. 57.

providing a parking place, any part of a recreation ground provided or maintained by it under section 8 of the Local Government Act 1894 (repealed in respect of recreation grounds by the Local Government Act 1972); or of an open space controlled or maintained by it under the Open Spaces Act 1906, other than a part which has been consecrated as a burial ground, or in which burials have taken place; or of any land provided by it as a playing field or for any other purpose under the Local Government (Miscellaneous Provisions) Act 1976 as amended.

No order under these provisions is to authorise the use of any part of a road so as unreasonably to prevent access to any premises adjoining the road, or the use of the road by any person entitled to use it, or so as to be a nuisance.

Various consents may have to be obtained. These are the same as those provided for several purposes in the Act of 1957 (*see* "Consents, etc. under the Parish Councils Act 1957"). The section also applies the same provisions relating to access to telegraphic lines, sewers, etc. as apply to bus shelters (*see* "Bus Shelters").

The parish council may employ with or without remuneration persons for the superintendence of parking places provided by them. They may make orders (subject to the consent of the county council) as to the use of such parking places, in particular as to the charges to be paid where the parking place is not part of a road.

A parking place which is not part of a road may be let for use as a parking place; but no single letting is to be for more than seven days (except as part of a letting under some other enactment of the land of which the parking place forms part).

The exercise of these powers does not render the parish council liable in respect of loss or damage to any vehicle parked in a parking place forming part of a road, or to its fittings or contents.

A parish council may contribute towards the reasonable expenses incurred by any person in providing a parking place, and towards the expenses of any other parish council in exercising these powers; and may combine with any other parish council for the purpose of exercising these powers.

A parish council may also maintain any parking place which could have been provided by them under this provision, but which was in fact provided, either by them before the commencement of the Act of 1957, or by some other person either before or after the said commencement.

A parish council may prosecute if heavy lorries are parked off a carriageway[1] and the police do not deal with the problem.

PARKS

(See Recreation)

PAROCHIAL CHARITY

(See Charities)

PAROCHIAL COMMITTEES

Parochial committees were abolished by the Local Government Act 1972.[2] There is a general power for a county, district or unitary council to delegate any of its functions to a parish council, whereupon the parish council acts as agent.[3]

---

[1] R.T.A. 1988, s. 19.

[2] By not reproducing L.G.A. 1933, s. 87.

[3] L.G.A. 1972, s. 101.

PASTURE

(*See* Common Pasture)

PATHS

(*See* Footpaths—Footways)

PECUNIARY INTERESTS

(*See* Interest in Contract or Other Matters)

PENSIONS FOR PAID OFFICERS

(*See* Superannuation of Paid Officers)

PETTY CASH

(*See* Accounts)

PHYSICAL TRAINING AND RECREATION, PROVISION FOR

(*See* Recreation)

PLANNING

(*See also* Untidy Land)

Generally speaking, under the Town and Country Planning Act 1990, as amended by the Planning and Compensation Act 1991, any development of land requires the prior permission of the planning authority. The county council is the planning authority for the county and the district council is the planning authority for the district. This apparently complicated statement is the result of the fact that certain planning powers are allocated to the county and some to the district, whilst others are concurrent powers exercisable by both. In most cases, however, planning applications are the responsibility of the district council. There is a right of appeal by an applicant to the Secretary of State against a refusal of permission to develop. If the parish falls within the area of a unitary authority (whether that be a county council or a district council), then that authority will be the planning authority.

The relevant planning authority is required to notify the parish council if the parish council informs that authority that it wishes to be notified of planning applications.[1] The authority is obliged to have regard to any comments made by the parish council, provided that they are made within fourteen days of the notification. If it is not possible to submit comments within this time limit, they should still be sent nevertheless, because there is no reason why the planning authority should not consider them, although after the time limit they are not obliged to do so. The planning authority is also required to inform the parish council of the result of the application or, if appropriate, of the date when the application was referred to the Secretary of State.[2] (On appeals, *see* "Public Inquiries".) An increasing number of planning authorities are now sending copies of plans to the parish councils in order to enable the parish councils to comprehend the likely effect of applications more readily and thus, in turn, to produce more informed and balanced comments from the parish councils.

Broadly speaking, "development" includes any building operation other than the maintenance or internal alteration of an existing building; and any material change in the use of any buildings or land, subject to certain exemptions.

---

[1] T.C.P.A. 1990, Sch. 1, para. 8 (England), Sch. 1A, para. 2 (Wales).
[2] Town and Country Planning (General Development Procedure) Order 1995, S.I. 419, Art. 13.

A "blanket" permission has been given by the Secretary of State to development of certain specified classes, subject to certain conditions, by the Town and Country Planning (General Permitted Development) Order 1995 (as amended).[1] For development within the scope of the Order, no separate application for permission is necessary. The classes of development covered by it include the erection by parish councils of certain "small ancillary buildings", which it is understood include lamp-posts, litter bins, bus shelters and roadside seats and shelters.

PLAYGROUNDS AND PLAYING FIELDS

(See Recreation—Village Greens)

PLEASURE GROUNDS

(See Recreation)

PLOUGHING OF PATHS

(See Footpaths)

POLLS

At a parish meeting, every question is decided in the first instance by the majority of those present and voting on the question, and the decision of the person presiding at the meeting as to the result of the voting is final, unless a poll is demanded.[2]

A poll may be demanded at any time before the conclusion of a parish meeting.[3]

---

[1] S.I. 1995, No. 418.
[2] L.G.A. 1972, Sch. 12, paras. 18(2) and 34(2).
[3] *ibid.*, paras. 18(4) and 34(4).

A poll, however, shall not be taken unless either the chairman of the meeting consents, or the poll is demanded by local government electors present at the meeting, not being less than ten in number or one-third of those present, whichever number is the less. The poll shall be taken on such day as shall be fixed by the returning officer, being a day not earlier than the fourteenth day or, unless for special reasons the Home Secretary otherwise directs, later than the twenty-fifth day after the day on which the poll was demanded.

Every poll consequent on a parish meeting is to be taken by ballot, in accordance with the Parish and Community Meetings (Polls) Rules 1987 as amended.[1]

The expenses of taking a poll are paid by the parish council.

As to the polls at the election of parish councillors, *see* "Election of Parish Councillors". As to polls relating to the creation, dissolution and grouping of community councils and communities, *see* "Parish Council – Creation and dissolution of community council in Wales *and* Grouping of parishes – Wales".

POLLUTION

(See Nuisances and Pollution)

PONDS

(See Ditches and Drains)

POOLS, SWIMMING

(See Baths, etc.)

---

[1] 1987, S.I. 1, as amended by 1987, S.I. 262.

POST-MORTEM ROOM

(See Mortuaries and Post-Mortem Rooms)

PRECEPTS

(See Expenses and Expenditure)

PRESERVATION OF TREES AND BUILDINGS

A parish council has no direct powers in these matters but may well wish to take an active interest in them. Both district and county councils have powers in respect of trees and buildings under the Planning Acts.

PRESS, ADMISSION OF, TO COUNCIL MEETINGS

(See Meetings of Parish Council)

PROCEEDINGS

(See Legal Proceedings—Parish Council—Parish Meeting—Public Inquiries)

PROPERTY OF PARISH COUNCIL

(See *also* Allotments—Community Centres—Compulsory Purchase—Damage—Information about Land—Public or Parish Offices—Recreation—Village Greens—Village Halls)

General

Parish property includes old parish workhouses and cottages provided by the overseers before the establishment of boards of guardians under the Poor Law Amendment Act 1834; lands acquired for the employment of the poor; vestry rooms; parochial offices; land allotted under an inclosure award to be used as village greens, recreation grounds, field gardens, or otherwise for the benefit of the inhabitants. Property formerly held by the board of guardians was transferred to the parish council by section 115 of the Local Government Act 1929.

The legal interest in all property which was formerly vested either in the overseers or in the churchwardens and overseers of the parish, other than property connected with the affairs of the church or held for an ecclesiastical charity, is vested in the parish council, subject to all trusts and liabilities affecting the same.[1]

All buildings, lands and hereditaments purchased, hired or taken on lease under the Poor Relief Act 1819, for the purpose of a workhouse or for the employment of the poor, and also other buildings, lands and hereditaments belonging to the parish are, therefore, vested in the parish council.

It should be observed, however, that the legal interest only is transferred to the council. The net income arising from the property should therefore be applied in accordance with the trusts upon which the property is held and, if it is applicable in aid of the rates, should be paid over to the council responsible for the collection of local government taxes.

Gifts

A parish council may accept, hold and administer any gift of property (other than a gift for an ecclesiastical charity, or a charity for the relief of the poor) for the purpose of discharging any of its functions, or for the benefit of the inhabitants of its parish, or of some part of it, and may execute any works

---

[1] L.G.A. 1894, s. 6.

(including works of maintenance or improvement) incidental to or consequential on these powers.[1]

Where such works are executed in connection with a gift for the benefit of the inhabitants of the local area (as contrasted with a gift directly related to one of the parish council's statutory powers, e.g. recreation), the cost of the works must come from the free resource. (*See* "Free Resource".)

As to the power of parish councils to provide suitable buildings for council business and public meetings, *see* "Public or Parish Offices".

Acquisition

A parish council may, by agreement, acquire by way of purchase, lease or exchange, any land, whether within or without its area, for the purpose of any of its functions under any public general Act of Parliament, or for the benefit, improvement or development of its area.[2] It may borrow money for purchasing any land which it is authorised to purchase. (*See* "Loans to Parish Council".) Where land is acquired, it is to be conveyed to the parish council as a corporate body.

As to compulsory purchase, *see* "Compulsory Purchase of Land."

A parish council is authorised to execute any works (including works of maintenance or improvement) in relation to any acquired land, but if the land was acquired for the benefit, etc. of its area, expenditure on works is limited to the free resource (*see* "Free Resource"). If, on the other hand, the land was acquired specifically for a statutory function, e.g. a playing field, there is no limit on the amount which may be spent.

[1] L.G.A. 1972, s. 139.
[2] L.G.A. 1972, s. 124.

A piece of land acquired for a specific purpose but not immediately required for that purpose, may be used temporarily for another purpose, so long as such use does not interfere with its use in due course for the purpose for which the land was acquired. It is not essential that during this time the land should be kept in the state which it was in when it was acquired.

Appropriation

Any land belonging to a parish council which is not required for the purpose for which it was acquired, or which has since been appropriated may be appropriated for any other purpose for which the council is authorised to acquire land by agreement.[1] There are procedural restrictions on appropriating common land and open spaces but, if these are satisfied, any public trust in the land ceases.

The consent of the Secretary of State is not required for appropriation except in the case of common land (which includes a town or village green) in excess of 250 square yards.

Appropriation may involve some adjustment in the accounts.

Letting

A parish council may let any land vested in it whether or not it is held for charitable purposes.[2] However, unless the lease is for seven years or less, the rent must be the best which can reasonably be obtained. If this is not so, the consent of the Secretary of State is required.[3] Land includes buildings, and the parish council thus has power to let any building vested in it.

---

[1] L.G.A. 1972, s. 126, as amended by L.G.P.L.A. 1980, Sch. 23, paras. 17 and 18.

[2] Ch.A. 1993, ss. 36 and 37.

[3] L.G.A. 1972, s. 127. The Secretary of State gave a general consent in January 1977 for any lease of land held for recreational purposes (*see* "Recreation").

Disposal

A parish council may sell any land it possesses. No Ministerial consent is required except that if land is sold for a consideration less than the best which can reasonably be obtained, the consent of the Secretary of State is necessary.[1] There are also certain restrictions on the disposition of charity land.[2] Capital money arising in cases other than the disposal of charity land may only be applied towards the discharge of debt or otherwise for capital purposes with the consent of the Secretary of State.[3]

Public trust land must not be sold unless the council gives notice in the local newspaper in two successive weeks and considers any objections which may be made to it. If such land is sold, it is freed from any trust arising solely because it is public trust land.[4]

Where, however, land has been purchased specifically for allotments, it is provided by the Allotments Act of 1925 that the parish council shall not sell, appropriate, use or dispose of the land for any other purpose without the consent of the Secretary of State (*see* "Allotments").

Parish councils are exempt from capital gains tax.

Protection of property

The parish council may incur expense in prosecuting or defending legal proceedings for the protection of property vested in it. For planning inquiries affecting such property, *see* "Public Inquiries".

If another local authority seeks to acquire compulsorily the property of a parish council and the council's objection is not

---

[1] L.G.A. 1972, s. 127.

[2] Ch.A. 1993, ss. 36 and 37.

[3] L.G.A. 1972, s. 153.

[4] L.G.A. 1972, s. 127(3) as substituted by L.G.P.L.A. 1980, Sch. 23, para. 19.

withdrawn, the acquisition may, in certain circumstances, be subject to special parliamentary procedure, as provided by the Acquisition of Land Act 1981. The Statutory Orders (Special Procedure) Acts 1945 and 1965 then apply. In brief, the proposal is examined at a local inquiry at which the parish council can state its case. It may further petition against the order which is then examined by a Joint Committee of both Houses of Parliament, at which the parish council can, if necessary, be represented by counsel. The costs of such representation may, of course, be substantial and the council would no doubt wish to take advice before incurring them.

Parish property, other than commons, village greens and recreation grounds irrevocably dedicated to the public, is liable to be rated for local non-domestic rates. (*See* "Rating and Valuation".) Income received by a parish council arising from parish property is exempt from income tax and corporation tax.

PROSECUTIONS BY PARISH COUNCIL

(See Legal Proceedings)

PUBLIC, ADMISSION OF, TO COUNCIL MEETINGS

(See Meetings of Parish Council)

PUBLIC BATHING, REGULATION OF

(See By-laws)

PUBLIC CLOCKS

A parish council is empowered to provide, maintain and light public clocks within the parish and to install them on or against any premises or in any other convenient situation.[1]

The exercise of this power is subject to provisions as to consents and access to telegraphic lines, etc.[2] (*See* "Consents, etc. under the Parish Councils Act 1957".)

A parish council may maintain a public clock provided by it before the commencement of the Act, or provided by any other person whether before or after such commencement; and may contribute towards the reasonable expenses of any other person, or the expenses of any other council, in the provision or maintenance of a public clock. An example is a church clock.

PUBLIC CONVENIENCES

A parish council has the power to provide public conveniences, provided that it does not place them in or under a highway or proposed highway without the consent of the highway authority, or district council if the latter is maintaining the highway.[3]

In providing such conveniences, the council has a duty to make provision, so far as is practical and reasonable, for the needs of disabled persons, and to display appropriate notices.[4]

PUBLIC GIFTS

(See Property of Parish Council)

---

[1] P.C.A. 1957, s. 2.
[2] As set out in P.C.A. 1957, s. 5.
[3] P.H.A. 1936, s. 87.
[4] Chronically Sick and Disabled Persons Act 1970, ss. 5, 7.

PUBLIC HEALTH

(See Ditches and Drains—Limits upon the Powers of the Parish Council)

PUBLIC INFORMATION

(See Information for the Public)

PUBLIC INQUIRIES

Many public inquiries, especially those into planning applications, are of considerable interest to a parish as a whole, and the parish council may wish to make representations in such cases. If they are taking a similar view to the county council or the district council, the best course may be for the chairman or clerk of the parish council to be called as a witness by whoever is presenting the other authority's case but, on occasion, the parish council may wish to represent its views separately, either because it takes a different view from the larger authority or for some other reason.

Planning appeals are normally concerned with questions of fact rather than law, and there is no rule that persons appearing at public inquiries must be legally represented. There are, however, cases where, for one reason or another, the parish council may consider that legal representation is desirable. Where the parish council's own property is affected, or the inquiry concerns the parish council as an authority, the council has an inherent right to incur necessary expenditure to defend its interests but, in all cases, the council has a statutory power to incur expenditure in appearing and representing its inhabitants at any public or other inquiry held by any ministry or public body under any Act.[1]

---

[1] L.G.A. 1972, s. 222.

PUBLIC NOTICES

(See Notices)

PUBLIC OR PARISH OFFICES

(See *also* Property of Parish Council—Rooms in School and Rooms Maintained Out of Rates)

In many of the larger parishes, vestry rooms or offices for the transaction of parochial business were acquired or erected by the overseers. Where such rooms or offices existed before the Local Government Act 1894 came into force, the legal interest in them passed to the parish council.

The powers of overseers to provide a vestry room or parochial room were transferred by the Local Government Act 1894 to the parish council. These powers are no longer required, as a parish council has a general power, without sanction from any government department (unless a loan is required), to provide or acquire and furnish buildings for transacting the business of the council, or of the parish meeting, or any other parish business,[1] and for public meetings and assemblies, or to contribute towards the expenses incurred by any other parish council or any other person in providing or acquiring and furnishing such a building.[2] The parish council may also move the district or unitary council to acquire compulsorily land for the purpose of providing or acquiring such buildings. (*See* "Compulsory Purchase of Land".)

Parish offices may be used by the council for entertainments, lectures, etc., or may be let to any person for the same purpose. Former restrictions on such use have been lifted. (*See* "Recreation".) The receipts from the occasional letting of a

---

[1] L.G.A. 1972, s. 111.
[2] L.G.A. 1972, s. 133.

room for concerts, etc. should be entered in the accounts of the parish council.

A council may borrow money for the purchase of land or for any building which the council is authorised to purchase or erect. (*See* "Loans to Parish Council".)

PUBLIC PATHS

(See Footpaths)

PUBLIC RIGHTS OF WAY

(See Highways)

PUBLIC WALKS

(See Recreation)

PUBLIC WORKS LOANS BOARD

(See Loans to Parish Council)

PUMPS

(See Water Supply)

QUALIFICATIONS FOR ELECTORS

(See Local Government Electors)

QUALIFICATIONS FOR OFFICE OF PARISH COUNCILLOR

(See Parish Councillor)

QUALITY PARISH COUNCILS

At the end of 2001, D.E.F.R.A. issued a consultation paper setting out how parish and town councils in England could seek "quality" status. The scheme was launched in March 2003. The main points of the scheme are, in summary, as follows.

The quality criteria

In order to attain quality parish status, a parish council must demonstrate that it has the attributes expected of a quality parish council and has the ability and capacity to take on the enhanced role and responsibility that quality status will bring. Tests have been devised to measure these criteria and cover the following:-

Test 1 – Electoral mandate

On first accreditation only: at least 80% of all council seats were filled at the beginning of the current four year term by members who stood for election at that time.

On re-accreditation: all council seats are filled at the beginning of the current four year term by members who stood for election at that time. This does not mean that there must be a ballot/election. "Stood for election" for the purposes of the quality scheme means councillors must have been nominated and stood as candidates. Where the number of candidates is the same as (or less than) the number of seats, then no ballot is held and candidates are automatically declared "elected" by the returning officer. In such cases, at least 80% of councillors must have been nominated and prepared to stand at the last round of elections in order to pass this test.

Test 2 – Qualifications of the clerk

The clerk to the council must hold one of the following qualifications:-

168

(a) Certificate in Local Council Administration awarded by the Assessment and Qualification Alliance (AQA); or

(b) Certificate of Higher Education in Local Policy or Local Council Administration awarded by the University of Gloucestershire.

The council should ensure that appropriate training and support is available to the clerk in order to help meet this test.

Test 3 – *Council meetings*

The council must meet on at least six occasions every year (the annual parish meeting may be counted as one of the meetings). Notices of the meeting must be publicly displayed at least three days before each meeting. Minutes of meetings must be available for inspection by electors. Time must be allowed at each meeting for public participation.

Test 4 – *Effective communication*

There are mandatory and discretionary elements to this Test. The mandatory requirements are as follows:–

Publication of regular information, perhaps in the form of a newsletter at least four times a year, including information on councillors and how they can be contacted, and a synopsis of the annual report. Information must be readily available at public sites across the parish. In addition, councils must meet at least nine of the discretionary requirements.

The discretionary elements comprise activities such as sending newsletters/annual reports to each household, maintenance of a parish council website, e-mail facilities, councillors' surgeries and consultation exercises.

Test 5 – *Annual report*

Publication of an annual report, including certain information, within a prescribed timescale and made readily available at sites across the parish.

Test 6 – Accountability

Accounts prepared in accordance with the requirements of the Accounts and Audit Regulations; unqualified accounts; adequate systems of internal control.

Test 7 – Ethical framework

Adoption of a local code of conduct (see Appendix 1).

The accreditation process

Applications for quality parish status will be vetted by panels at county level, which will be established by the National Association of Local Councils (N.A.L.C.) in consultation with stakeholders including the Local Government Assocaition and the Society of Local Council Clerks and approved by O.D.P.M. and D.E.F.R.A. N.A.L.C.'s county associations will service the panels.

O.D.P.M. and D.E.F.R.A. will approve a panel's membership where they are satisfied that the panel will collectively have experience and knowledge of both principal local authorities and parish councils.

Where the panel decline to confer quality parish status, the council will be told why and the panel will indicate the specific improvements that are expected and a date after which it will be possible to apply again for quality parish status.

Successful parish councils will receive a certificate confirming their quality parish status for four years and will be able to use the quality parish council logo during this period. Parish councils will be required to re-apply every four years to keep their quality parish status.

A small fee will be charged to cover the costs of the accreditation process.

The scheme does not apply in Wales. The National Assembly has commissioned a study of the powers and functions of community councils. When this has been completed, the Assembly will no doubt decide what changes, if any, are desirable.

QUORUM

There is no rule which provides for a quorum at a parish meeting. In the case of a parish council, the quorum is one third of the total number of members of the council, but with the qualification that in no event must the quorum be less than three.[1] If, for some reason, more than one third of the members of the council are disqualified at the same time, the quorum is to be calculated by taking one third of the number of members remaining qualified, again with the qualification that there is a minimum of three.[2]

RATING AND VALUATION

Parish councils have no responsibility either for valuation or for the collection of rates or other local taxes.

In most cases, the district or unitary council is the responsible authority for raising local taxes, including rates on non-domestic property (see Local Government Finance Act 1988). If there is any income for the benefit of the parish paid to the district or unitary council, it reduces the overall charge levied in the parish.

Agricultural land and agricultural buildings are exempted from rates. Agricultural land includes allotments and allotment gardens.

---

[1] L.G.A. 1972, Sch. 12, paras. 12 and 28.
[2] *ibid.*, para. 45.

Also exempt are parks, recreation grounds, open spaces, etc. provided by, or under the management of, a local authority (which includes a parish council or parish meeting) and available for use by members of the public.

Parish councils will doubtless assure themselves that the valuation list exempts property of these kinds in which they are interested. They may also be concerned with the eligibility for rate relief of certain property. There is mandatory relief for 80% of the full rates on property occupied by a charity and wholly or mainly used for charitable purposes; and rating authorities have discretionary power to allow further relief of up to 100% for a range of organisations including sports clubs. Although these measures do not normally extend to property occupied by parish councils, relief is permissible if the council is occupying the property as trustees.

Domestic property is subject to the council tax, not to non-domestic rates (*see* "Council Tax"). Parish councils cannot precept on non-domestic rates.

READING AND RECREATION ROOMS

(See Public or Parish Offices)

RECORDS

(See Books and Documents)

RECREATION

(See *also* By-laws—Commons—Community Centres— Expenses—Open Spaces—Roadside Seats and Shelters —Swimming Pools—Tourism—Village Greens)

Pleasure grounds, parks and public walks

A parish council has power to acquire land for a pleasure

ground, park or a public walk. It may purchase or take on lease, lay out, plant, improve and maintain lands for these purposes and may maintain or contribute to the maintenance of these facilities provided by any person.[1] The council may make by-laws for the regulation of any such land which is under its control, or to the expense of which it has contributed. Any by-laws must be confirmed by the Secretary of State (usually, but not always, the First Secretary of State). The council may, on such days as it thinks fit (not exceeding twelve days in any one year, or six consecutive days on one occasion) close any such land or part thereof to the public and may grant the use of it, either free or for payment, to any public charity or institution, or for any agricultural, horticultural, or other show or other public purpose, or may use the ground itself for any such show or purpose. Not more than one quarter of the total available public pleasure land may, however, be closed on any Sunday or public holiday. The admission to the ground on any closed day may be either with or without payment.[2]

The council may either itself provide and let for hire, or license any person to let for hire, any pleasure boats on any lake or piece of water in any such pleasure ground and may make by-laws regulating the same. It may also provide a boating pool, the boats and any equipment reasonably required for this purpose.[3]

Playing fields, recreational facilities and centres

A parish council is empowered to provide inside or outside its area such recreational facilities as it thinks fit, including the provision of buildings, equipment, supplies and assistance of any kind. These powers are very wide and cover all kinds

---

[1] P.H.A. 1875, s. 164, and L.G.A. 1972, Sch. 14, para. 27.
[2] P.H.A.A.A. 1890, s. 44, and P.H.A. 1961, s. 53.
[3] P.H.A. 1961, s. 54.

of indoor and outdoor recreations, e.g. tennis courts, squash courts, swimming pools,[1] etc. The facilities may be provided free or for such charges as the council considers appropriate.[2] The facilities may be let to voluntary organisations.[3] The Secretary of State may make grants to voluntary organisations towards capital expenditure under the Act for purposes of physical training and recreation. Parish councils may obtain grants from county or district councils or from the National Playing Fields Association, 25 Ovington Square, London, SW3 1LQ. Another useful contact is Sport England, 16 Upper Woburn Place, London, WC1H 0QP. The address of the Sports Council for Wales is National Sports Centre, Sophia Gardens, Cardiff, CF1 9SW. (*See* "Grants".)

Premises provided for recreational purposes may be used by the parish council for concerts or other entertainments which may be provided by the council or by any other person; and they may be let for these purposes, or for meetings.

The county council and the district council have concurrent powers for the same purpose; and a parish council may contribute (either by way of grant or loan) towards the expenses incurred by another local authority, or by a voluntary organisation, in providing or maintaining any facility which the parish council may provide. Similarly, another local authority may contribute to the expenses of the parish council.

For powers to acquire land compulsorily, *see* "Compulsory Purchase of Land".

A recreation ground which is irrevocably dedicated to the

---

[1] As to swimming pools, *see* "Baths, Wash-houses, Swimming Pools and Bathing Places".

[2] L.G.(M.P.)A. 1976, s. 19.

[3] L.G.A. 1972, s. 127. The Secretary of State gave a general consent for such lettings in January 1977.

public is not rateable, provided that on the actual facts of the case it can be shown that the public is the true occupier. As to the rating of playing fields, *see* "Rating and Valuation".

REFUSE

(See Litter)

REORGANISATION OF PARISHES

(See Alteration of Areas—Grouping of Parishes)

REPRESENTATIVE BODY

(See Parish Trustees)

RESIGNATION

(See Chairman of Parish Council—Parish Councillor)

RESOLUTION

(See Meetings of Parish Council)

RETIREMENT FROM OFFICE

(See Parish Councillor)

REVIEW OF BOUNDARIES

(See Alteration of Areas)

RIGHTS OF WAY

(See Footpaths—Highways)

ROADS

(See *also* Consents, etc. under the Parish Councils Act 1957—Ditches and Drains—Highways—Lighting— Parking Places—Roadside Seats and Shelters— Roadside Waste)

For the purposes of the provisions of the Parish Councils Act 1957 and the Road Traffic Regulation Act 1984, relating to lighting, parking places and seats and shelters in roads, "road" is defined[1] as meaning any highway (including a public path) and any other road, lane, footway, square, court, alley or passage (whether a thoroughfare or not) to which the public has access, but does not include a special road (as defined by the Highways Act 1980).[2]

ROADSIDE DITCHES

(See Ditches and Drains)

ROADSIDE SALES

(See Highways)

ROADSIDE SEATS AND SHELTERS

(See *also* Bus Shelters)

A parish council may provide and maintain seats and shelters for the use of the public and install or erect them in proper and convenient situations in, or on any land abutting on, any road within the parish.[3]

For the definition of "road", *see* "Roads".

---

[1] P.C.A. 1957, s. 7, and R.T.R.A. 1984, s. 60(4).
[2] H.A. 1980, s. 16.
[3] P.C.A. 1957, s. 1.

The exercise of the powers is subject to various consents[1] (*see* "Consents, etc. under the Parish Councils Act 1957"), and to the same provisions relating to access to telegraphic lines, sewers, etc. as apply to bus shelters (*see* "Bus Shelters").

A parish council may combine with any other parish council for the joint exercise of these powers;[2] may contribute towards the expenses of any parish council in the exercise of the powers;[3] and may contribute towards the reasonable expenses of any person in doing anything which the council is empowered to do under these provisions.[4]

The parish council may also maintain any seat or shelter which could have been provided by it under these provisions but was in fact provided either by it before the commencement of the Act or by some other person either before or after the said commencement.[5]

As to borrowing for this purpose, *see* "Loans to Parish Council".

Planning permission is not required for the provision of seats and shelters (*see* "Planning").

ROADSIDE VERGES

(See Highways—Roadside Wastes)

ROADSIDE WASTES

Where on either side of a public road strips of land exist open to the public, between the metalled road and the fences

---

[1] P.C.A. 1957, s. 5.
[2] L.G.A. 1972, s. 101(5).
[3] P.C.A. 1957, s. 6(1).
[4] *ibid.*
[5] P.C.A. 1957, s. 6(2).

beyond, *prima facie* the public right of way extends, unless there is evidence to the contrary, over such strips of roadside wastes, and they cannot lawfully be enclosed by the owner of the adjoining land, or by the lord of the manor, or by any other person.

Such strips may be of varying width, and the adjoining owner has no right to straighten the line of his fences by taking in any part of the roadside waste. The public, in the absence of proof to the contrary, have the right to the whole of the roadside waste between the fences and the metalled road. The fact that trees or shrubs have been allowed to grow upon these roadside wastes so as to interfere with their use by the public does not destroy such right or justify the enclosure of any such wastes.

A parish council which considers that a roadside waste has been unlawfully encroached upon, may make representations on the subject to the district or unitary council which then has a duty to take proceedings on the matter, unless satisfied that the allegations are incorrect.[1] Roadside waste was not registrable under the Commons Registration Act 1965.

In certain cases the courts have held that a parish council has a right to let the herbage on the roadside wastes.[2] The right must be established by evidence of ancient custom, or grant under a parish award or otherwise.

ROOMS IN SCHOOL AND ROOMS MAINTAINED OUT OF RATES

(See *also* Meetings of Parish Council—Public or Parish Offices)

Where there is no suitable public room vested in the parish

---

[1] H.A. 1980, s. 130.
[2] A.G. *v. Garner* [1907] 2 K.B. 480.

council or parish trustees which can be used free of charge, a suitable room in a school maintained by a local education authority, or a suitable room, the expense of maintaining which is payable out of any rate, may be used free of charge at all reasonable times and after reasonable notice for any of the following purposes:-

(a) a parish meeting or any meeting of the parish council; or

(b) meetings convened by the chairman of the parish meeting in England or by the parish council; or

(c) the administration of public funds within or for the purposes of the parish where these funds are administered by any committee or officer appointed, either by the parish meeting or by the parish council or by a county or district council.[1]

The use of any room used as part of a private dwelling-house such, for instance, as the teacher's residence, is, however, not authorised.

The school hours of a day or evening school must not be interfered with. Care should be taken to select a time which will cause the least possible inconvenience to the persons responsible for the conduct of the school.

This freedom from charge relates to expenses in the nature of rent. It does not necessarily extend to freedom from charge for services rendered in connection with the use of the room, such as heating, lighting or cleaning or, as indicated below, the repair of damage.

In the case of a room used for the purposes of the administration of justice, or for the purposes of the police,

---

[1] L.G.A. 1972, s. 134.

there must be no interference with the hours during which the room is used for those purposes.

If any question arises as to what is "reasonable" or "suitable", it is to be determined, in the case of a school room, by the Secretary of State for Education and Skills; in the case of a room used for the purposes of the administration of justice, or for the purposes of the police, by the Home Secretary; and in any other case, by the Secretary of State.

As to what is "reasonable notice", the Secretary of State for Education and Skills advises that (except as regards some meetings of parish councils) the notice should be served not less than seven clear days before the date named and that, in most cases, longer notice, as a rule not less than fourteen days' notice, should be given. As regards meetings of parish councils, three clear days' notice would ordinarily suffice for a special parish council meeting but longer notice should, if possible, be given.

Any expense incurred for damage or otherwise in connection with the use of the room must be defrayed, in the case of an inquiry as part of the expenses of the inquiry, and in any other case as expenses of the parish meeting or parish council.

A candidate at an election of a parish councillor is entitled, for the purpose of holding public meetings in furtherance of his candidature, to the use free of charge at reasonable times between the last day on which notice of the election may be published and the day preceding the day of election, of a suitable room in the premises of a community, foundation or voluntary school situated in the electoral area for which he is a candidate (or if there is no such school in that area in any such school in an adjacent electoral area) or in a parish or community in part comprised in that electoral area.[1]

---

[1] R.P.A. 1983, s. 96, as substituted by R.P.A. 1985, Sch. 4, as amended by the School Standards and Framework Act 1998, Sch. 30, para. 11.

A parish council may also make standing orders with respect to the making of contracts by the council. However, it *must* make such orders with respect to contracts for the supply of goods or materials to the council, or for the carrying out of any works, which orders must include a provision for regulating the manner in which tenders are invited, but may exempt from any such provision contracts below a certain fixed price or, generally, where the council is satisfied that exemption is justified by special circumstances.[1]

Model standing orders are obtainable from the National Association of Local Councils, 109 Great Russell Street, London, WC1B 3LD.

STATUTORY NUISANCES

(See Noise—Nuisances and Pollution)

STILES OR GATES, REPAIR OF

(See Footpaths)

STOPPING UP OF A HIGHWAY

(See Highways)

STREAM

(See Water Supply)

STREET FURNITURE, DAMAGE TO

(See Damage)

---

[1] L.G.A. 1972, s. 135.

STREET LIGHTING

(See Lighting)

SUBSCRIPTIONS TO ASSOCIATIONS

There is a specific power for a parish council to pay a reasonable subscription to the funds of any association of local authorities formed (whether inside or outside the United Kingdom) for the purpose of consultation as to the common interest of those authorities and the discussion of matters relating to local government. The parish council may also pay subscriptions to the funds of any associations of members or officers of local authorities formed for the like purposes.[1]

Subscriptions to associations other than local government associations may be paid out of the free resource (*see* "Free Resource").

SUBSISTENCE ALLOWANCES

(See Allowances to Parish Councillors)

SUCCESSOR COUNCIL

(See Parish Council)

SUPERANNUATION OF PAID OFFICERS

In those cases in which the salary paid to an officer of the council is his sole or main source of income and his services are full-time, it may be desirable to make provision for his superannuation. This can be done through the appropriate superannuation fund usually maintained by the county council,

---

[1] L.G.A. 1972, s. 143.

by a statutory resolution of the parish council (specifying each officer covered).[1] At least 28 days' public notice must be given of the terms of the resolution and the fact that it will be moved at the meeting.

The broad principle of the statutory scheme is that percentage deductions are currently made from the officer's salary, with corresponding contributions payable by the council, into the superannuation fund. Upon retirement, subject to certain conditions, a pension is payable out of the fund based on the officer's average annual remuneration in his final years of service.

Other benefits which may be obtained include widows' pensions (subject to a reduction of the retirement grant) and death grants.

Where a pension is not payable, a parish council can, at its discretion, award an officer upon retirement a gratuity.[2] This may be a lump sum, or an annuity up to the amount specified under the 1996 Regulations. This charge falls directly upon the council's funds and not upon the superannuation fund. Such a gratuity can be paid to a part-time employee.

The foregoing is no more than a brief sketch. It is subject to various qualifications in respect of the relevant service and the calculation of the amounts.

SWIMMING POOLS

(See Baths, etc.)

TAX

(See Income Tax—Value Added Tax)

---

[1] L.G. Pension Scheme Regulations 1995, S.I. 1019, Reg. B1(i).
[2] L.G. (Discretionary Payment) Regulations 1996, S.I. 1680.

TERM OF OFFICE OF PARISH COUNCILLORS

(See Election of Parish Councillors)

THIRD PARTY RISKS

(See Insurance)

TITHE APPORTIONMENT AND MAP

(See Books and Documents)

TOMBSTONES

(See Burial and Cremation)

TOURISM

(See *also* Recreation)

A parish council has power to encourage persons to visit its area, by advertisement or otherwise, for recreation, health purposes, conferences, trade fairs and exhibitions. It may provide, or encourage other persons or bodies to provide, facilities for conferences, trade fairs and exhibitions. It may also improve, or encourage other persons or bodies to improve, any existing facilities for these purposes.[1]

TOWN AND COUNTRY PLANNING

(See Planning)

---

[1] L.G.A. 1972, s. 144 as amended by L.G.(M.P.)A. 1976, ss. 19(5), 81(1), and Sch. 2.

TOWN COUNCIL

Any parish council, which is not subject to a grouping order, may itself resolve that the parish will have the status of a town, whereupon the council becomes the town council, the chairman and vice-chairman of the council are entitled to the style of town mayor and deputy town mayor, and the parish meeting becomes the town meeting.[1] Such an arrangement does not require the consent or approval of any other council or of the Secretary of State.

TOWN MAYOR

(See Chairman of Parish Council—Town Council)

TRAFFIC CALMING

(See Highways)

TRANSPORT

Car-sharing schemes

A parish council may establish a car-sharing scheme for the benefit of people in the council's area, or assist others in so doing.[2]

Grants for bus services

A parish council may make grants to any body which operates bus services for the elderly or disabled, or a community bus service, for the benefit of people in the council's area.[3]

Taxi fare concessions

A parish council may enter into arrangements with a licensed

---

[1] L.G.A. 1972, s. 245(6).
[2] L.G.R.A. 1997, s. 26.
[3] Transport Act 1985, s. 106A, inserted by L.G.R.A. 1997, s. 27.

taxi operator whereby the council reimburses the operator the cost of running a fare concession scheme for residents in the council's area who are eligible to receive travel concessions.[1]

Information about transport

A parish council may (a) investigate the provision and use of public passenger transport in its area, (b) the use of and need for roads in its area, and (c) the management and control of traffic in its area. It may also publicise information about public passenger services in its area.[2]

TRAVEL ALLOWANCES

(See Allowances to Parish Councillors)

TREASURER OF PARISH COUNCIL

(See *also* Accounts—Deputy Officers—Employees)

The parish council may appoint one of its members to take the office of treasurer without remuneration,[3] but nowadays it is usual to employ an officer for this purpose.[4] Frequently the offices of clerk and treasurer are combined. In all cases a parish council must ensure that one of its officers has responsibility for the administration of its financial affairs.[5]

The council must take from its treasurer such security for the faithful execution of his office as the council considers sufficient.[6] The parish council must defray the cost of the security. Every such security must be produced at audit.

---

[1] L.G.R.A. 1997, s. 28.
[2] L.G.R.A. 1997, s. 29.
[3] L.G.A. 1972, s. 112(5).
[4] L.G.A. 1972, s. 112(1) and (2).
[5] L.G.A. 1972, s. 151.
[6] L.G.A. 1972, s. 114.

Every cheque or other order for the payment of money by the parish council must be signed by two members of the council.[1]

Like the clerk of a parish council, the treasurer must disclose any interest which he has in any contract of the council. (*See* "Clerk of Parish Council".)

TRUSTEES

(See Charities—Parish Trustees)

TRUSTEE SECURITIES

(See Investment)

UNHEALTHY DWELLINGS

(See Housing)

UNTIDY LAND

(See *also* Information about Land—Litter)

Under the Town and Country Planning Act 1990,[2] a planning authority may serve on the owner of untidy land a notice requiring him to take appropriate steps to tidy up the land. Failure to comply with the notice may result in a fine of up to level 3 on the standard scale for summary offences (currently £1,000) and to a further fine of up to £40 per day for continued failure to comply after conviction. Furthermore, the planning authority who served the notice may enter the land and itself carry out the necessary work, charging the cost to the owner.

---

[1] L.G.A. 1972, s. 150(5).
[2] T.C.P.A. 1990, s. 215.

Parish councils can report cases to the planning authority with a request for action to be taken as above.

The Secretary of State has power to make grants for the purpose of reclaiming, improving or bringing into use derelict land.[1]

VALUATION LISTS

(See Rating and Valuation)

VALUE ADDED TAX

Value added tax (V.A.T.) is charged essentially on the supply of goods and services in the United Kingdom and on the importation of goods into the United Kingdom.[2] The administration of the tax is under the control of H.M. Customs and Excise.

A parish council must register with the appropriate Customs and Excise Office if it supplies, or expects to supply, any goods or services for which payment is made by the recipient (other than wholly through rates) which fall within the definition of "taxable" supply. A supply of goods or services is a "taxable" supply if it is either standard rated or zero rated.

H.M. Customs and Excise supply notices which should be obtained by any parish council wishing to study the implications of V.A.T. for the activities of the council.[3]

Examples of services which a parish council may supply which might require V.A.T. to be taken into account include matters relating to cemeteries, recreation, entertainments, highways, parking places, etc. Certain activities are, however, exempted.

---

[1] Derelict Land Act 1982, s. 1.
[2] Value Added Tax Act 1994, s. 1.
[3] Numbers 749 and 749A.

Value added tax

The basic or standard rate of value added tax is currently 17.5%. This can be changed up or down within certain limits by a Treasury order without Parliamentary approval.[1] This standard rate must be charged by a local council on any service or goods supplied. Certain services and goods are zero rated (see leaflet No. 749). The local council must, nevertheless, technically charge value added tax at zero rate on the provision of these services or goods. These charges, i.e. at standard rate or zero rate, are called the output tax and must be clearly shown in the accounts.

Once it has been established that a supply is to be rated for value added tax (whether at standard or zero rate), the local council may then *deduct* any tax which it itself paid, e.g. on purchase of goods before supplying them, or on services rendered to the council in connection with the subsequent supply (i.e. the input tax—also to be clearly shown in the accounts). The balance between the output tax recovered by the local council and the in-put tax paid is then to be paid to H.M. Customs and Excise.

In addition, a parish council, whether registered as above or not, is entitled to *recover* any *in-put* tax paid by the council in respect of any goods or services acquired by the council for any non-business activity, e.g. the tidying up of grass verges. A registered parish council may do this on form VAT 100 on a monthly basis. A non-registered council should apply periodically to H.M. Customs and Excise, 2nd Floor, Alexander House, Southend-on-Sea, Essex, SS99 1AU.

There are special rules covering supplies of goods and services which are exempt, or partly exempt, from V.A.T. (see V.A.T. Notice 749) and for the disposal or acquisition of land and property (see V.A.T. Notice 742 "Land and Property"). Specialist advice on these matters should normally be sought.

---

[1] Value Added Tax Act 1994, s. 2.

VERGES, ROADSIDE

(See Highways—Roadside Wastes)

VICE-CHAIRMAN

(See Chairman of Parish Council)

VILLAGE GREENS

(See *also* Commons—Open Spaces—Recreation— Roadside Seats and Shelters)

At the end of the eighteenth century a large number of inclosures were authorised by local Inclosure Acts. In satisfaction of the rights of the inhabitants over the land inclosed, the local Act usually provided that some portion of the land should be awarded or allotted (hence the term "allotment") to the church-wardens and overseers of the parish in which it was situate, either for the benefit of the poor (e.g. as a place for cutting fuel) or as a place of recreation for the inhabitants, such as a village green or recreation ground. The general Inclosure Act of 1845 enabled a village green to be allotted to the church-wardens and overseers in trust to allow the same to be used for the purposes of exercise and recreation.

Apart from village greens allotted to the church-wardens and overseers, there are many such greens in parishes in which no inclosure was made, usually consisting of waste of the manor, on which the inhabitants of the parish have a customary right exercised for not less than 20 years to play games. Such custom constitutes land as village green and, except by failure to register under the Commons Registration Act 1965, the inhabitants cannot lawfully be deprived, by inclosure or otherwise, of their right so to use it.[1] It is

---

[1] *New Windsor Corporation v. Mellor* [1975] 3 All E.R. 44.

sometimes useful to bear in mind that the availability of a village green is to the inhabitants of the parish and not to the public in general.

Village greens, in many cases, are vested in and managed by the parish council for the benefit of the inhabitants. Under the Commons Registration Act 1965, land constituting a village green where ownership is unclaimed vests in the parish council.[1]

The parish council may ask the district council to make by-laws for the regulation of any village green which is for the time being under their control, or to the expense of which they have contributed. The by-laws cannot take effect until they have been confirmed by the Secretary of State. (*See* "By-laws".)

A parish council may purchase or take on lease, lay out, plant, improve and maintain lands for the purpose of being used as village greens, and may support or contribute to the support of land available for public use provided by any person whomsoever.[2]

A parish council must not allow a village green which it owns to be encroached upon or to be misused. If the problem is keeping vehicles off, this can usually best be achieved by digging a ditch or putting large white stones on the boundary or fencing the green (provided there is reasonable access for pedestrians). If the ownership of the green is not vested in the parish council, it will be necessary first to obtain the owner's consent. Land which is registered as village green cannot be used for car parking or caravan parking, even if the council wishes, because it is unlawful for the land not to be kept freely available for the inhabitants of the parish for lawful sports and pastimes.

---

[1] Commons Registration Act 1965, s. 8.
[2] P.H.A. 1875, s. 164, and L.G.A. 1972, Sch. 14, para. 27.

A parish council must not, except as provided by s. 68 of the Countryside and Rights of Way Act 2000 (see next paragraph), grant a private vehicular access over any village green which it owns, since such use is incompatible with the council's duty to preserve the status of the land for recreational purposes.

Under s. 68 of the Countryside and Rights of Way Act 2000 and the Vehicular Access Across Common and Other Land (England) Regulations 2002 (S.I. 1711), a statutory easement (right of way) may be created where someone uses a vehicular access to a property over land where it is an offence to drive, but otherwise the use would be sufficient to create an easement. The Regulations set out the procedure to be used and specify the amount of compensation payable to the owner of the land over which the claimed access way runs. Section 68 will apply only to those access ways where a prescriptive right of way could otherwise be claimed. Thus an applicant for a statutory easement will in practice have to be able to show a sufficient period of unchallenged use to meet the conditions set out in the Prescription Act 1832 or under the doctrine of lost modern grant, i.e., in broad terms, 20 years.

At the time of writing (April 2003), no regulations for Wales had been made.

The parish council, with the usual consents, may borrow money to purchase land for the purpose of being used as a village green. (*See* "Loans to Parish Councils".) The land could be acquired compulsorily. (*See* "Compulsory Purchase of Land".)

Encroachment on a village green with a defined boundary is a public nuisance and can be dealt with as such by the magistrates on the information of the parish council. Any person who wilfully injures a village green or interferes with its use as a place of recreation can be prosecuted and, if found guilty, fined up to level 1 on the standard scale for summary offences (currently £200.) He may also be required to pay for the damage caused.[1] This may be a useful weapon against persons unlawfully parking on greens.

VILLAGE HALLS

There is a wide power available to a parish council to provide and equip suitable buildings as village halls or centres for clubs, societies or organisations having athletic, social or educational objects.[2] The council may manage such buildings with or without charge for their use or for admission, or may let them, or any portion, at a nominal or other rent to any person, club, society or organisation for use for any of the aforesaid purposes. (*See* "Recreation".) It is usual for a representative organisation, a "Community Association", to undertake the management of the building.

A parish council may also contribute to the expenses of providing or maintaining a community centre incurred by another local authority (e.g. the district or unitary council, who may provide a centre for a new housing estate in the parish under the Housing Act 1985[3]) or by a voluntary organisation, such as a Community Association. The parish council may act as trustee for a community centre provided by a voluntary organisation. Where the parish council acts as trustee for a community centre (but not where they provide one themselves as a local authority), it may be possible to claim rate relief as a charity (*see* "Rating and Valuation").

A parish council may be able to obtain a grant from the county, unitary or district council or through A.C.R.E. (*see* "Grants"). It may be possible to raise part of the cost from voluntary

---

[1] Inclosure Act 1857, s. 12.

[2] L.G.(M.P.)A. 1976, s. 19.

[3] Housing Act 1985, s. 12.

sources. In some areas, voluntary labour has been used. Capital expenditure falling on the parish council may be raised by borrowing (see "Loans to Parish Council").

VOTING

(See Election of Parish Councillors—Meetings of Parish Council)

WALES ASSOCIATION OF COMMUNITY AND TOWN COUNCILS

The Wales Association of Community and Town Councils is an independent association for community and town councils. Its address is Unit 5, Betws Business Park, Park Street, Ammanford, SA18 2ET.

WARDS

(See *also* Alteration of Areas—Parish Meeting)

Where a parish has a relatively large population, or where the population is scattered over a wide area, making it difficult to find a convenient place for a meeting of all the local government electors, or where one parish contains two or more sections with separate interests, e.g. a parish which comprises a section with a population distinctly agricultural in its pursuits and another area with a manufacturing or seafaring population, it may be convenient to divide the parish into wards for the purpose of electing councillors. In England, the procedure is governed by Part II of the Local Government and Rating Act 1997, which empowers a district or unitary council to review electoral arrangements within its area and to make any necessary changes. Guidance is given in the Department of the Environment, Transport and the Regions'

Circular 11/97 "Local Government and Rating Act 1997 – Parish Reviews". In Wales, the procedure is governed by section 57 of the Local Government Act 1972, which places a duty on county and county borough councils to keep under review the electoral arrangements for communities in their area. On a request by a community council, or at least 30 electors in a community, the Local Government Boundary Commission for Wales may review the electoral arrangements for the community, including whether or not the community should be divided into wards.

The wards will have such boundaries and such number of councillors for each ward as may be prescribed by the order made by the district or unitary council.

Where a parish is divided into wards, the parish councillors for each ward are elected in the same manner as councillors are elected for a parish. The rules relating to the election of councillors apply to each ward as if it were a parish. The parish councillors for all the wards will form only one parish council, and there will still be a parish meeting for the whole parish for purposes other than the election of councillors. A casual vacancy among parish councillors is filled by the whole parish council.

Where a parish is divided into wards, no local government elector may sign a nomination paper for, or vote in, more than one ward in connection with the election of councillors. There is a separate part of the register of the local government electors for each ward of a parish.

WAR MEMORIALS

Generally, a parish council may accept, hold and administer gifts of property, real or personal, for the benefit of the inhabitants of the parish, or some part of it, and may execute any works (including works of maintenance or improvement) incidental to or consequential thereto.[1] This power may be drawn upon, for example, to enable a parish council to have transferred to it a war memorial originally purchased by voluntary subscriptions.

Another statutory power enables a parish council to incur expenditure in the maintenance, repair and protection of any war memorial within the parish whether it is vested in the council or not.[2] A council may thus fence the memorial and repair the fence when necessary. This power was amended in 1948 to enable a parish council also to incur expenditure in the alteration of any such memorial so as to make it serve as a memorial in connection with any war subsequent to that in connection with which it was erected, or to have corrected any error or omission in the inscription on any such memorial.[3]

WASTE LAND AND WASTES

(See Roadside Wastes—Untidy Land—Village Greens)

WATERCOURSES

(See Ditches and Drains—Nuisances and Pollution)

WATER SUPPLY

(See *also* Ditches and Drains)

A parish council may utilise any well, spring or stream within its parish and provide facilities for obtaining water therefrom, and may execute any works, including works of maintenance

---

[1] L.G.A. 1972, s. 139(1).

[2] War Memorials (Local Authorities' Powers) Act 1923, ss. 1 and 3.

[3] L.G.A. 1948, s. 133.

or improvement, incidental to, or consequent on, any exercise of this power.[1] The power does not authorise it to interfere with the rights of any person; nor does it restrict, in the case of a public well or other works, any powers of the district or unitary council with reference to public pumps, wells, cisterns, reservoirs, conduits and other works used for the gratuitous supply of water to the inhabitants of any part of the district, all of which vest in the district council.[2]

A parish council may contribute towards the expenses incurred by any other parish council, or by any other person, in doing anything authorised by the provision above summarised.

Thus, a parish council has very limited powers of providing a water supply for its parish. It has no authority to incur any expense in bringing water from outside the parish. A parish council is not empowered to carry out any works of magnitude involving the laying of mains, the construction of reservoirs, etc. These powers are within the province of the water undertaker, which also has the requisite powers for breaking up streets, charging water rates, etc.

Where access to a public well by the inhabitants of a parish is prevented, the parish council cannot take proceedings for the purpose of restraining interference with the access of the public to the well, as the well is vested in and under the control of the district or unitary council and it would be for that council to take action to recover damages for interference with the access of the public to the well, or for an injunction to restrain such interference. Where, however, damage is done to a well, e.g. by removing or injuring the cover to a well provided by the parish council, the parish council could bring an action for damages against the person who removed or injured the cover.

---

[1] P.H.A. 1936, s. 125.
[2] P.H.A. 1936, s. 124.

Appendix I

MODEL CODE OF CONDUCT FOR PARISH COUNCILS

Part I
GENERAL PROVISIONS

Scope

1.–(1) A member must observe the authority's code of conduct whenever he:–

  (a) conducts the business of the authority;

  (b) conducts the business of the office to which he has been elected or appointed; or

  (c) acts as a representative of the authority,

and references to a member's official capacity shall be construed accordingly.

(2) An authority's code of conduct shall not, apart from paragraphs 4 and 5(a) below, have effect in relation to the activities of a member undertaken other than in an official capacity.

(3) Where a member acts as a representative of the authority:–

  (a) on another relevant authority, he must, when acting for that other authority, comply with that other authority's code of conduct; or

  (b) on any other body, he must, when acting for that other body, comply with the authority's code of conduct, except and insofar as it conflicts with any other lawful obligations to which that other body may be subject.

201

(4) In this code:-

    (a) "member" includes a co-opted member of an authority; and

    (b) "responsible authority" means a district council or a unitary county council which has functions in relation to the parish councils for which it is responsible under section 55(12) of the Local Government Act 2000.

General obligations

2. A member must:-

    (a) promote equality by not discriminating unlawfully against any person;

    (b) treat others with respect; and

    (c) not do anything which compromises or which is likely to compromise the impartiality of those who work for, or on behalf of, the authority.

3. A member must not:-

    (a) disclose information given to him in confidence by anyone, or information acquired which he believes is of a confidential nature, without the consent of a person authorised to give it, or unless he is required by law to do so; nor

    (b) prevent another person from gaining access to information to which that person is entitled by law.

4. A member must not in his official capacity, or any other circumstance, conduct himself in a manner which could reasonably be regarded as bringing his office or authority into disrepute.

5. A member:-

(a) must not in his official capacity, or any other circumstance, use his position as a member improperly to confer on or secure for himself or any other person, an advantage or disadvantage; and

(b) must, when using or authorising the use by others of the resources of the authority:

   (i) act in accordance with the authority's requirements; and

   (ii) ensure that such resources are not used for political purposes,

   unless that use could reasonably be regarded as likely to facilitate, or be conducive to, the discharge of the functions of the authority or of the office to which the member has been elected or appointed.

6. A member must, if he becomes aware of any conduct by another member which he reasonably believes involves a failure to comply with the authority's code of conduct, make a written allegation to that effect to the Standards Board for England as soon as it is practicable for him to do so.

Part 2
INTERESTS

Personal interests

7.–(1) A member must regard himself as having a personal interest in any matter if the matter relates to an interest in respect of which notification must be given under paragraphs 12 and 13 below, or if a decision upon it might reasonably be regarded as affecting to a greater extent than other council tax payers, ratepayers, or inhabitants of the authority's area, the well-being or financial position of himself, a relative or a friend or:–

(a) any employment or business carried on by such persons;

(b) any person who employs or has appointed such persons, any firm in which they are a partner, or any company of which they are directors;

(c) any corporate body in which such persons have a beneficial interest in a class of securities exceeding the nominal value of £5,000; or

(d) any body listed in sub-paragraphs (a) to (e) of paragraph 13 below in which such persons hold a position of general control or management.

(2) In this paragraph:–

(a) "relative" means a spouse, partner, parent, parent-in-law, son, daughter, step-son, step-daughter, child of a partner, brother, sister, grandparent, grandchild, uncle, aunt, nephew, niece, or the spouse or partner of any of the preceding persons; and

(b) "partner" in sub-paragraph (2)(a) above means a member of a couple who live together.

Disclosure of personal interests

8. A member with a personal interest in a matter who attends a meeting of the authority at which the matter is considered must disclose to that meeting the existence and nature of that interest at the commencement of that consideration, or when the interest becomes apparent.

Prejudicial interests

9.–(1) Subject to sub-paragraph (2) below, a member with a personal interest in a matter also has a prejudicial interest in that matter if the interest is one which a member of the public with knowledge of the relevant facts would reasonably regard as so significant that it is likely to prejudice the member's judgement of the public interest.

(2) A member may regard himself as not having a prejudicial interest in a matter if that matter relates to:–

(a) another relevant authority of which he is a member;

(b) another public authority in which he holds a position of general control or management;

(c) a body to which he has been appointed or nominated by the authority as its representative;

(d) any functions of the authority in respect of statutory sick pay under Part XI of the Social Security Contributions and Benefits Act 1992, where the member is in receipt of, or is entitled to the receipt of such pay from a relevant authority; and

(e) any functions of the authority in respect of an allowance or payment made under sections 173 to 173A and 175 to 176 of the Local Government Act 1972 or section 18 of the Local Government and Housing Act 1989.

Participation in relation to disclosed interests

10. A member with a prejudicial interest in any matter must:–

(a) withdraw from the room or chamber where a meeting is being held whenever it becomes apparent that the matter is being considered at that meeting, unless he has obtained a dispensation from the standards committee of the responsible authority; and

(b) not seek improperly to influence a decision about that matter.

11. For the purposes of this Part, "meeting" means any meeting of:–

(a) the authority; or

(b) any of the authority's committees, sub-committees, joint committees or joint sub-committees.

Part 3
THE REGISTER OF MEMBERS' INTERESTS
Registration of financial and other interests

12. Within 28 days of the provisions of an authority's code of conduct being adopted or applied to that authority or within 28 days of his election or appointment to office (if that is later), a member must register his financial interests in the authority's register maintained under section 81(1) of the Local Government Act 2000 by providing written notification to the monitoring officer of the responsible authority of:–

(a) any employment or business carried on by him;

(b) the name of the person who employs or has appointed him, the name of any firm in which he is a partner, and the name of any company for which he is a remunerated director;

(c) the name of any person, other than a relevant authority, who has made a payment to him in respect of his election or any expenses incurred by him in carrying out his duties;

(d) the name of any corporate body which has a place of business or land in the authority's area, and in which the member has a beneficial interest in a class of securities of that body that exceeds the nominal value of £25,000 or one hundredth of the total issued share capital of that body;

(e) a description of any contract for goods, services or works made between the authority and himself or a firm in which he is a partner, a company of which he is a remunerated director, or a body of the description specified in sub-paragraph (d) above;

(f) the address or other description (sufficient to identify the location) of any land in which he has a beneficial interest and which is in the area of the authority;

(g) the address or other description (sufficient to identify the location) of any land where the landlord is the authority and the tenant is a firm in which he is a partner, a company of which he is a remunerated director, or a body of the description specified in sub-paragraph (d) above; and

(h) the address or other description (sufficient to identify the location) of any land in the authority's area in which he has a licence (alone or jointly with others) to occupy for 28 days or longer.

13. Within 28 days of the provisions of the authority's code of conduct being adopted or applied to that authority or within 28 days of his election or appointment to office (if that is later), a member must register his other interests in the authority's register maintained under section 81(1) of the Local Government Act 2000 by providing written notification to the monitoring officer of the responsible authority of his membership of or position of general

control or management in any:–

(a) body to which he has been appointed or nominated by the authority as its representative;

(b) public authority or body exercising functions of a public nature;

(c) company, industrial and provident society, charity, or body directed to charitable purposes;

(d) body whose principal purposes include the influence of public opinion or policy; and

(e) trade union or professional association.

14. A member must within 28 days of becoming aware of any change to the interests specified under paragraphs 12 and 13 above, provide written notification to the monitoring officer of the responsible authority of that change.

Registration of gifts and hospitality

15. A member must within 28 days of receiving any gift or hospitality over the value of £25, provide written notification to the monitoring officer of the responsible authority of the existence and nature of that gift or hospitality.

Note: The Welsh equivalent to the foregoing regulations is contained in the Conduct of Members (Model Code of Conduct) (Wales) Order 2001.

Appendix 2

FORMS AND RECORDS

published by
SHAW & SONS LIMITED
for the use of
LOCAL COUNCILS
(Parish Councils, Town Councils
and Community Councils)

*All the documents listed on the following pages may be
ordered from:*

Shaw & Sons Limited
Shaway House
21 Bourne Park
Bourne Road
Crayford
Kent DA1 4BZ

Tel: 01322 621100
Fax: 01322 550553
E-mail: sales@shaws.co.uk

*Further information about all Shaw's products and services can
be found at*
www.shaws.co.uk

Catalogue No.	Description

Accounts

PC 6 **Receipts and payments book**
specially designed to provide the information required by the Financial Statements (Parishes) Regulations, comprising:–
    6 pages Burial Grounds Account
    16 openings General Accounts
    4 pages Charities Account
    4 pages Allotments Account
    2 openings Loans and Sales of Assets Account
page size 14" x 9"

PC 6G **Receipts and payments book**
with blank column headings *book of 50 leaves*

PC 6A **Annual receipts and payments book**
with blank headings *manilla covered book of 12 openings*
(this is particularly suitable for small parishes and will enable accounts to continue to be kept in a new volume each year whilst the previous year's book is with the auditors)

PC 12 **Assets register** *bound book of 24 openings*
manilla covered book of 12 openings

PC 13B **Parish council receipt book** *book of 100 in duplicate*

LD **General receipt book** *book of 100 in duplicate*

AG 18 **Allotment garden rent receipt book**, two entries per leaf
book of 50 in duplicate

AG 7 **Allotment rent book** *book of 25 leaves*

AG 20 **Allotment rent book** *book of 100 leaves*

BUR 32A **Burial fees receipt book** *book of 50 in duplicate*

BUR 22 **Burial fees account book** *book of 50 leaves*
book of 100 leaves

Allotment Gardens

AG 2A **Application for allotment garden** (model form)

AG 6F **Agreement for letting** (model form) – full form

Catalogue No.	Description

AG 4   **Notice of determination of tenancy**
under s.30 of the 1908 Act

AG 5   **Register of allotment gardens**, with columns for
particulars of tenancy, etc.   *book of 50 leaves*

AG 7   **Allotment rent book**   *book of 25 leaves*

AG 20   **Allotment rent book**   *book of 100 leaves*

AG 18   **Allotment garden rent receipt book**, two entries per leaf
book of 50 in duplicate

ALLOWANCES TO LOCAL COUNCILLORS

CLG 17   **Application for attendance or financial loss allowance**

CLG 16   **Application for travelling and subsistence allowance**

CLG 18L   **Record of allowances paid**   *loose-leaf sheets, 13" x 14"*

AUDIT

LG 11   **Notice of audit** for parish council, community council or
town council

BOOKS AND DOCUMENTS

QS 1   **Register of deeds**
book of 100 leaves, with index cut through fore-edge

QS 1L   **Ditto**   *loose-leaf sheets, 8³/₈" x 14"*

QS 2   **Index to papers**   *loose-leaf sheets, 8³/₈" x 14"*

BURIAL AND CREMATION

REGISTERS RELATING TO GRAVES

BUR 3A   **Register of graves** – general pattern (6 grave spaces per
page)   *book of 100 pages*
book of 200 pages

BUR 3B   **Register of graves, combining register of grants of
exclusive right of burial** (8 grave spaces per page)
book of 100 pages
book of 200 pages

Appendix 2

Catalogue No.	Description

BUR 12 **Register of public graves in consecrated ground**
(8 grave spaces per page) *book of 100 pages*

BUR 13 **Register of public graves in unconsecrated ground**
(8 grave spaces per page) *book of 100 pages*

BUR 4 **Register of purchased graves**
(8 grave spaces per page) *book of 100 pages*
book of 300 pages

GRANTS OF EXCLUSIVE RIGHT OF BURIAL

BB 24 **Grant of exclusive right of burial**
book of 50 in duplicate
book of 100 in duplicate
*Grants can also be printed to order incorporating local
particulars. Please enquire for details.*

BUR 35 **Register of grants of exclusive right of burial**
book of 50 openings

BUR 3B **Register of graves, combining register of grants of
exclusive right of burial**
(8 grave spaces per page) *book of 100 pages*
book of 200 pages

BUR 17 **Assignment of exclusive right of burial**

BUR 16 **Register of transfers of exclusive right of burial**
book of 100 pages

REGISTERS RELATING TO BURIALS AND MORTUARIES

BUR 6 **Register of burials** (8 names per opening)
book of 50 openings
book of 100 openings
book of 150 openings

BUR 11 **Index to register of burials**
book of 50 leaves, with index cut through foredge

BUR 10 **Register of disinterments** (8 names per opening)
book of 25 openings
book of 50 openings

DC 52 **Mortuary register** *book of 25 leaves*
book of 50 leaves

Forms and records

Catalogue No.	Description
	NOTICES AND CERTIFICATES
BUR 29	**Notice to burial authority of intended interment**
INT 13	**Notice to clergyman to attend funeral** *book of 100, with counterfoil*
INT 14	**Notice to sexton to prepare grave** *book of 100, with counterfoil*
	MISCELLANEOUS
BUR 7	**Certified extracts from the register of burials** *book of 50*
BUR 32A	**Receipts for interment fees paid** *book of 50 in duplicate*
BUR 22	**Burial fees account book** *book of 50 leaves* *book of 100 leaves*
	BOOKS OF CONDOLENCE
IM 1	**In memoriam condolence book** *book of 100 leaves*
IM 2	**In memoriam condolence book** *book of 50 leaves*
	CREMATIONS
BUR-G	**Register of cremations** *book of 50 leaves*
BUR-P	**Register of cremation of body parts** *book of 50 leaves*
CRE 7	**Certified extracts from the register of cremations** *book of 50*
	FORMS RELATING TO THE ERECTION OF MONUMENTS
BUR 36	**Application for grant of right to erect and maintain, or add inscription to, memorial**
BUR 37	**Grant of right to erect and maintain, or add inscription to, memorial**, with copy for cemetery superintendent *book of 50 in duplicate*
BUR 34	**Register of memorials** (8 entries per opening) *book of 50 openings*

ELECTION OF LOCAL COUNCILLORS

Comprehensive list of forms relating to the election of Councillors will be supplied on request.

Catalogue No.	Description

Employees

CERTIFICATES OF APPOINTMENT, etc.

RF 3   **Official certificate of appointment by local authority**
folding card to be carried by officer

RF 11   **Ditto** – with provision for photograph

RF 4   **Authority to enter premises** (general form)
folding card to be carried by officer

RF 9   **Ditto** – with provision for photograph

        Wallets for above are available individually

RF 2   **Personal record sheet**
comprising a comprehensive record of the following details
in respect of each individual:–
      (a) personal particulars
      (b) record of service
      (c) details of previous local government service
      (d) special assessment and annual report
      (e) examination successes and qualifications
      (f) grading
      (g) record of salary and allowances
      (h) details of overtime worked
      (i) record of annual leave, sick leave and other absences
loose-leaf sheets, 13" x 16$\frac{1}{2}$"

RF 8   **Personal record sheet**
alternative pattern   *loose-leaf sheets, 8$\frac{3}{8}$" by 14"*

RF 8A   **Personal record of sickness and leave**
continuation sheet to RF 8

HS 40   **Record book of reportable injuries, dangerous
occurrences and reportable cases of disease**
manilla covered book in two sections

OFFICERS' EXPENSES

RF 5   **Log book** for officers using own cars for official purposes
book of 23 openings

RF 6   **Claim for subsistence allowance and travelling expenses**

IB 1C   **"Ideal" permanent cover** for log book

Forms and records

Catalogue No.	Description

DISCLOSURE BY OFFICERS OF INTEREST IN CONTRACTS

CLG 27   **Notice by officer of pecuniary interest in contract or proposed contract**

CLG 24   **Register of disclosures by officers of pecuniary interest in contracts or proposed contracts**

EXPENDITURE

PC 5   **Precept by parish council upon district council**
book of 25 in duplicate

TC 5   **Precept by town council upon district council**
book of 25 in duplicate

CC 5   **Precept by community council upon county/county borough council**   *book of 25 in duplicate*

JB 14   **Precept by joint committee upon district council**
book of 25 in duplicate

LAND

ML 33   **Requisition for information as to persons interested in land** (Local Government (Miscellaneous Provisions) Act 1972, s.16)

ML 33A   **Ditto** – with tear-off reply form attached

LITTER

LIT 1   **Dropping of litter – information**

LIT 2   **Ditto – summons**

LOCAL COUNCILLORS

CLG 11   **Notice of vacancy in office** of councillor

PC 9   **Public notice of vacancy in office** of parish councillor

TC 9   **Public notice of vacancy in office** of town councillor

CC 9   **Public notice of vacancy in office** of community councillor

PCE 34   **Notice to person elected** as parish councillor

Catalogue No.	Description
WE 34	**Notice to person elected** as community councillor
LE 40	**Declaration of acceptance of office** by chairman or councillor *single form*
LE 40/1	**Declaration of acceptance of office** by chairman or councillor *book of 100 entries*
LE 40/2	**Ditto** *book of 200 entries*
EW 40	**Declaration of acceptance of office** by chairman or councillor – **bilingual Welsh/English**
EW 40/1	**Ditto** *book of 100 entries*

MODEL CODE OF CONDUCT (ENGLISH REGULATIONS)

LGA 1 **Notification by member of a local authority of financial or other interests**

LGA 2 **Notification by member of a local authority of receipt of gift or hospitality** over the value of £25

LGA 3 **Notification by member of a local authority of change of registered financial or other interests**

LGA 10 **Register of members' financial or other interests**
loose-leaf sheets, 13" x 16^1/$_2$"

NETA(8) **"Neta" loose-leaf binder**, to hold above sheets

LGA 10A **Register of members' financial or other interests** – as above but in book form suitable for parish councils
manilla covered book of 50 openings

LGA 11 **Register of gifts or hospitality received by members**
manilla covered book of 25 openings

CODE OF CONDUCT (WELSH REGULATIONS)
Please note these forms are written in English but conform to Welsh legislation

LGA 1W **Notification by member of a local authority of financial or other interests**

LGA 2W **Notification by member of a local authority of receipt of gift, hospitality, benefit or advantage**

LGA 3W **Notification by member of a local authority of change of registered financial or other interests**

Catalogue No.	Description

LGA 10W **Register of members' financial or other interests**
loose-leaf sheets, 13" x 16$^1/_2$"

NETA(8) **"Neta" loose-leaf binder**, to hold above sheets

LGA 10AW **Register of members' financial or other interests** – as above but in book form suitable for community councils
manilla covered book of 50 openings

CODE OF CONDUCT (WELSH REGULATIONS)
Please note these forms are written in Welsh

LGA 1W* **Notification by member of a local authority of financial or other interests**

LGA 2W* **Notification by member of a local authority of receipt of gift, hospitality, benefit or advantage**

LGA 3W* **Notification by member of a local authority of change of registered financial or other interests**

MEETINGS OF LOCAL COUNCIL

PARISH COUNCILS

PC 3B **Public notice of annual meeting** of parish council

MC 1P **Notice to councillor of annual meeting** of parish council
A5 size

PC 4 **Ditto** (alternative pattern) *A4 size*

PC 2M **Public notice of ordinary meeting** of parish council

PC 2 **Notice to councillor of ordinary meeting** of parish council *A5 size*

PC 3 **Ditto** (alternative pattern) *A4 size*

TOWN COUNCILS

TC 2 **Public notice of annual meeting** of town council

TC 3 **Notice to councillor of annual meeting** of town council
A5 size

TC 4 **Ditto** (alternative pattern) *A4 size*

TC 6 **Public notice of ordinary meeting** of town council

Appendix 2

Catalogue No.	Description

TC 7   **Notice to councillor of ordinary meeting** of town council
           A5 size

TC 8   **Ditto** (alternative pattern)   *A4 size*

COMMUNITY COUNCILS

CC 2   **Public notice of annual meeting** of community council

CC 2W   **Ditto – Welsh language version**

CC 3   **Notice to councillor of annual meeting** of community
council   *A5 size*

CC 3W   **Ditto** – Welsh language version   *A5 size*

CC 4   **Ditto** (alternative pattern)   *A4 size*

CC 4W   **Ditto** – Welsh language version   *A4 size*

CC 6   **Public notice of ordinary meeting** of community council

CC 6W   **Ditto – Welsh language version**

CC 7   **Notice to councillor of ordinary meeting** of community
council   *A5 size*

CC 7W   **Ditto** – Welsh language version   *A5 size*

CC 8   **Notice to councillor of ordinary meeting** of community
council (alternative pattern)   *A4 size*

CC 8W   **Ditto** – Welsh language version   *A4 size*

RECORDS OF MEETINGS

HM 20   **Attendance register** for signature by councillors,
with summary   *book of 50 leaves*

HM 21   **Ditto – summary form**
with columns for recording attendances   *book of 50 leaves*

HM 22   **Motion book** for entering notices of motions
to be made at meetings   *book of 50 leaves*

PC 1   **Minute book**, with rules as to meetings and proceedings
of parish meetings, parish councils and committees printed
in front, numbered and indexed   *book of 150 leaves*

CC 1   **Minute book**, with rules as to meetings and proceedings
of community meetings, community councils and
committees printed in front, numbered and indexed
         book of 150 leaves

Catalogue No.	Description

MIN A4   **Minute book** – a four post semi-lockable binder which takes standard A4 punched paper

Parish or Community Meetings

PM 2   **Public notice of annual parish meeting**

PM 3   **Public notice of ordinary parish meeting**

TM 2   **Public notice of annual town meeting**

TM 3   **Public notice of ordinary town meeting**

CM 3   **Public notice of community meeting**

CM 3W   **Ditto – Welsh language version**

For minute books, etc., see Meetings of Local Council

Property of Local Council

DC 63   **Register of properties** belonging to the council
loose-leaf sheets, 13" x 11$\frac{1}{4}$"

Recreation Facilities

A 16H   **Council room or hall lettings book**   *book of 25 leaves*
book of 50 leaves

Seal

DC 12C   **Seal register** with index at front, numbered 1-51
book of 50 leaves
     Ditto – numbered 1-101   *book of 100 leaves*